FACING LIFE
AFTERCOLLEGE

A compulsory recipe to all graduants

N. MICHAEL

Table Of Contents

Dedication.

I dedicate this book to all people engaged in business, innovators and those who are planning to join entrepreneurship.
I also dedicate it to all students in colleges and universities.
May God guide your paths; you are the hope for our great nation and rich Africa.

Acknowledgements

I am grateful to God the Almighty for once again giving me an opportunity and energy to write this inspiring and life-changing book.

Am grateful to my family; to my wife Gladys and my lovely daughters Joy and Salome. Thank you so much for allowing me time to sit for long hours as I toiled to make this idea a reality. Thank you.

Heartfelt appreciation to my relatives, and especially my Mum and my brother peter for their encouragements. Am always grateful for your unwavering support and love.

Thanks also to my church P.C.E.A Joseph Ngwaci for its spiritual nourishment that continues to inspire my journey and my life even in business matters and writing.

Special thanks to my mentors in my entrepreneurial journey who have greatly inspired my writing to a great length with their great innovations, perseverance and success in their entrepreneurial journeys. Specifically I would like to appreciate Dr. S. K. Macharia of Royal Media Services for his handwork, perseverance and courage that has culminated to success. His life story has inspired the writing of this volume to a great degree. I would also like to appreciate the contribution of Jack Ma, the founder of E-commerce Giant Alibaba for his inspiring story of innovation. His life struggles is a great lesson to upcoming innovators in Africa.

I also cannot forget to appreciate the great work of innovative Kenyans whose stories have been featured in this book. Vitalis Kiplagat with his great innovation of a multi-functional candle, Roy Allele and his amazing innovation that introduced Sign-10 in the world, The Milele Alliance and their success story in Chama Business, Mr Paul Mbugua of Kuza and his great advice on farming options in a ¼ acre piece of land and finally our great Safaricom Limited for its mobile money transfer innovation that has transformed lives in Kenya and beyond.

I would also like to thank everyone who has taken part in ensuring the success of this book. Not forgetting the great work of editors who have worked tirelessly to make sure they deliver a quality masterpiece. Thank you all.

PREFACE

"**Facing Life after College**"means to have a plan on how a graduate from high school, college or university can face the realities of life after leaving school. Most graduates usually have unrealistic expectations on how life is outside their university or college time zone. While few may be lucky to sail through and get into employment without major hurdles, majority find themselves stranded. This book is therefore geared towards addressing this hurdle of the majority who after graduations finds themselves in the face of unforgiving monster called unemployment. The most amazing thing about this book is that, while the book focuses mainly on guiding those who find it hard to secure formal employment, it does not leave behind the ones who get into employment but still interested in entrepreneurship.

As a teacher who has taught in primary and secondary schools for more than a decade, I could not help seeing, my most brilliant students waste away due to lack of formal employment after leaving college. The problem here is not the graduants but the slow economic growth of most African economies due to rampant corruption, nepotism, tribalism and ignorance. For so long, our best brains have been wasted through unemployment and much worse, a brain drain by the developed nations. What is left of us is a nation without innovators and great thinkers. The results are endless strives and useless tribal battles for the few resources that end up making the situation worse. The solution to all these challenges is coming up with a model of guiding all graduates on how to face this unforgiving monster of unemployment. This book is product of such ideologies.

With a guide on how to conduct oneself after graduation and the various options available for them, it is left to the discreation of the graduates to make a choice. What I would personally hate to see is desperation and hopelessness among our graduates and young people due to unemployment.

One of the greatest lessons we can learn from China is innovation. Innovation policies in China is what has led to its big manufacturing capacity. With a big manufacturing capacity comes employment and wealth. If African countries including Kenya will not adopt such policies, our development agenda will not go far. This book suggests that our graduates have the capacity to change the dark story and history of Africa to a success one if guided accordingly. What is the best methodology of offering such guidance? It is offering information on various options available for them plus real life stories about others who have made it in such ventures. This book therefore focuses on passing this information.

Why this book is designed for you

If you are an entrepreneur or a college/university student considering building a product or engaging in business, this is the right prescription for you. The book is expertly designed to direct your way on how to start your business, how to face life after college/university and how you can make it in your innovation. If you have already started, it shows you how to grow immensely until you hit the multinational status. In short, "Facing Life after College" is designed for the following people.

- ❖ Starters and those planning to start business.
- ❖ Innovators and those already in different stages of innovation.
- ❖ Employed people who are finding it hard to start investment.
- ❖ All School leavers: college/university leavers and high school dropouts.
- ❖ Programme developers interested in becoming successful entrepreneurs.
- ❖ Teachers and motivational speakers.
- ❖ Religious leaders dealing with youths and career counsellors.

Why this Book.

It is very important to note that this book is not your conventional entrepreneurship book filled with all manner of Western theories and complex calculations that are never applicable to our African business culture and models. This book can only be described as "a unique assortment filled with African's entrepreneurial stories and inspirations." Although there are few stories from elsewhere in the planet, they have been carefully crafted to fit our Kenyan and African business models.

This book gives you a chance to interact with real life stories of ordinary people from various backgrounds who have risen from nothing to something. Unlike books from European world that rarely relate with our African style of business and challenges, this book creates a unique platform for the reader to relate with local examples. To make it even more interesting, the book contains a challenge segment that calls for the reader's response and participation. Moreso, it highlights specific lessons learned after each chapter, something that makes it interactive and educative.

I wrote this book with the intention of helping thousands of students who are graduating from various cadre of our educational system but finding themselves in a world full of hurdles that they are less prepared to face. My greatest aim being shaping their lives and encouraging them that they have all it takes to make it in life. I have also not forgotten those who are employed in both public and private institutions as the book has also outlined ways of venturing into business when still employed. For me my advice to the reader is; read it for information, guidance, inspirations and most importantly put into practice the knowledge that you acquire from it.

INTRODUCTION.

THE PILOT WHO MADE A BOAT.
How a Misfortune turned up to be a business Idea.

Sometimes back, a family set out for a holiday vacation in a foreign country. The rich family owned a small aircraft which they used for travel. On the set day, the small aircraft with the pilot, his wife and two sons set out for the journey. They had to fly over a certain sea before getting into the country of their destination. After frying for some hours over the beautiful sea, the weather suddenly changed; there were thick dark clouds, heavy rain, blinding lightning and thunderstorms. There was also poor visibility and the pilot could not see clearly. The small aircraft could not withstand the sudden change in weather. The pilot started losing control of it. What followed was great panic as the plane was now at the mercy of a violent storm. Disoriented by the bad weather condition, the plane started to stall and within minutes, they were crashing. It crashed on top of huge trees in an abandoned island in the middle of nowhere. Luckily, nobody got serious injuries and the family was able to disembark safely. The aircrafts wings and engine however were badly damaged. It was some hours before dusk and it was still raining heavily. The family walked around looking for shelter and spotted an old house structure. There they spent their first night.

They following day, the family had no food to eat apart from a few chocolates they had carried for the kids. Inside the old structure was an old fishing net and some rusted cooking pots. It seemed that some anglers had abandoned it there. It was torn, so they repaired it and used it to get some fish from the sea. They washed the pots and prepared the fish. They were therefore able to survive for the second day on the abandoned island as they hoped to be rescued.

On the third day, the lastborn son was coughing, sneezing and complaining of severe headache. The boy could not eat. Everything was now turning from bad to worse and no rescuer was forthcoming. That day, the pilot tried everything he knew to try to get attention from the outside world, but nothing positive was forthcoming. By evening, the son's condition had worsened. "Dad, if you don't make a boat for us to escape this place, we are all going to fall sick and die in this island," The eldest son complained after observing his brother's condition.

That night, the pilot did not sleep. He turned and turned wondering how he was going to get his family out of the dangerous island. By morning, he had a solution. He ventured into the forested area of the island, dug and uprooted several medium sized trees and tied them together using ropes made from some tree barks. By noon, the pilot had placed his whole family on his improvised boat heading to the main land, which was approximately thirty kilometres from the mainland according to his map. After sailing for about an hour in the cold waters, a fishing boat located them and came to their aid. The pilot would later narrate his ordeal to the media, how a misfortune caused him to make a boat from nothing.

"I have to realize that, when faced with danger, you can even make an aeroplane and escape especially when your life and that of your loved ones, is in danger," he said to one of the media house. The millionaire later opened a motor boat manufacturing industry, something that has earned him wealth and respect.

"Before I had no interest in sea and boats, but that incident made me develop great interest in boat manufacturing and sea safety equipment" said the pilot to one of the business magazines years later after the incident.

My Advice.

As you begin reading this book, you could be in a situation similar to that of this family. They could have blamed the weather, lose hope and die in that dangerous island. But the father decided to fight for his sick son who was on the verge of death and for the future of his family. At the end, they all emerged victorious, and a business opportunity came about from that misfortune. I urge you to fight on, for your dignity, for your children, for your future, for your well-being and that of the society.

Chapter One

THE MEANING OF
LIFE AFTER COLLEGE

During graduation, everything looks fantastic: friends, relatives' gifts, flowers, encouraging messages et al. The problem is that most of the people who attend your graduation will rarely tell you that life outside college is difficult. Prayers will be part of this graduation, most people asking God to give you a good job so that you can take good care of your parents and probably your younger siblings. Some will give you tips on how to spend your money once you secure a job, a job you have no idea where it will come from.

No one cares to talk about starting your own business if for any reason you do not secre a job. This means that from day one, your mind is focused on only one thing: job seeking, or white-collar job.

Lesson from my school principal - Man is Always in Chains

The first few days of freedom come as a relief after graduation, as you are vacationed in cerebrating a new world free of stressful exams and nagging lectures. However, this freedom does not last long before you start wondering what you are supposed to do next.

I can vividly recall what my principal told us when we completed our high school education. Clearing his throat loudly, he said, "Some of you are already celebrating the fact that you have completed your high school education, that you are free at last from our numerous school rules and regulations. But now, you have entered into **another school of life** where if you break the rules, the state will be on you. Initially my teachers and I used to punish you for the mistakes you did while in school but from

12

now hence forth, **the state** will be handling your discipline matters. **Man is always in chains.** You have come out of one prison of responsibility and are now entering into another prison of even greater possibility." He thanked us for everything and wished us success in the future. That was many years ago.

Something stuck in my mind: *"man is always in chains."* According to me, he was trying to say that we are always chained in our responsibilities. When I therefore went through college and university, I always knew that I had been chained in my responsibilities including the responsibility of wanting to succeed in everything I did.

After some days of staying at home after graduation, you will also realize that you are also chained in your responsibility of wanting to succeed in life. Challenged by this passion, the first thing that comes to your mind is waking up and looking for a job.

You prepare your best CV ever and start dropping papers everywhere in those big multinational companies. One month later, you get no reply. The second month is when several letters of regret come through, some of them too daring to state;

> Dear sir/madam
> We are very sorry to inform you that you did not meet the criteria set by our selection panel. You can always look for other opportunities in our company in future.
>
> Thank you for considering working with us.
> Yours faithfully."

You feel discouraged and frustrated, so you lower your standards and start targeting small and medium scale companies. However, as well, there is nothing forthcoming. That is the time you start appreciating the small guys who own kiosks, shops, restaurants et al. You also realize that you are not alone in this hustle: you are in your thousands. Nevertheless, as the Bible stipulates, **"Every man has to work for him to eat."** You are now ready to work anywhere so that you can **"eat."**

My brother's Big Lesson
All good things come to those who wait (English Proverb)

When my brother got into the university, he was beside himself with joy. "What an opportunity!" And for sure, a university or college education is such a great opportunity for everyone who is eager to change their life. So in his third year, as iusual, they were to go for attachment. He was very positive, and since he had awesome grades both in high school and university, getting an internship opportunity would be a walk over. He thought. He started looking for internship in big companies, big banks and multinational organisation but there were no a response. He turned to small and medium scale firms, but still there was no answer. He started getting very frustrated and stressed. He had hoped to work in those multinational organisations, but as it were, enen the small firms were hesitant in engaging him. He was not even looking for a job: he was looking for an attachment.

Lecturers were calling to check if all the students had secured attachments. Some had, but the likes of my brother had not. It was then that he had to swallow the humble pie and get advice on areas and companies where he was likely to get the attachment. He therefore consulted friends and relatives until he finally got an opportunity with a major dairy company. Since he is a B.com person, he got a chance to work in the financial department.

"What a relief! On the ground, things could be very different, he discovered. He therefore worked diligently: a workhorse during the internship period, something that earned him a legacy of "the most industrious intern in the company". At the end of his internship, he got not only a good recommendation letter from his supervisors but also word that he should report to the same company after graduation. That was a lucky shot.

After Graduation.

After graduation, he was very lucky to emerge victorious and graduate with honours. He had also completed his CPA. To say the least he was "ripe for the market". He prepared himself for the next landing. He got some new clothes using his savings and, of course, the money he had gotten from friends and relatives during graduation. He also armed himself with a magnificent CV and headed to the company as he had been promised a year earlier. The boss at the Dairy Firm appreciated seeing him back, but also regretted that there was no permanent employment by then. He was therefore asked if he could be willing to work on contract basis as a clerk, with the promise that if employment opportunity emerges, he would be the first to be considered.

The salary was less than KSh. 20,000. "What! A B.com graduate who had completed his CPA?" But considering what the young man had encountered when he was looking for internship, he accepted the offer and hoped for the best. The company's hardworking intern was now the company's clerk. Doing all simple and complex duties that the ordinary clerks could not handle. Since he would complete his light duties before noon, most of the time, the company was forced to give him extra work or overtime jobs Therefore, for most afternoons and evenings he was being assigned other senior accounting jobs. These overtime jobs helped to boost his earnings while still being viewed as a clerk on contract basis. He faithfully worked for the company while still looking for greener pastures, connecting with friends and working online in the evening and on weekends.

The Great "Opening"

One day, his expected opportunity showed up on the Daily Nation Newspaper. The company was looking to hire senior accountants in the head office. My brother had the qualifications needed - B.com graduate and CPA with at least two years' experience. He had worked for the company for almost a year and he had done a commendable job during the internship period.

According to him, he was one-step away from the finishing line - hefty salary, house allowance and more importantly, a permanent and pensionable status. He drafted an elaborate CV and quoted the vast experience he had gained in the company's various departments and beyond. In his application letter, he never forgot to mention that he had developed a cordial relationship with his colleagues. He knew the boss, and the boss knew his work and fine qualities. His supervisors were also very positive that Peter was going to get a job. Encouragements were all over.

The D-day and the Greatest Disappointment.

On the D-day, my brother was clad in a black suit. He attended the interview as usual. The questions were fine, as he had always been a smart person; to say the least, the interview was just fine. The results were supposed to be out after three weeks. He expectantly waited with patience and passion of joining the company on permanent basis terms. It was his longest wait. Finally "the bombshell!" He was neither in the list of senior nor junior accountants. Concisely he was nowhere. That day he contemplated the worst in his career. Quitting. "Enough is enough." But before then, he took some time to do some soul searching. He went home earlier that day, and since it was on Friday, he pondered over the matter over the weekend. The new "qualified" workers who had been hired were to report the following Monday. They are going to be my bosses, he wondered. Finally, after making several prayers, Peter decided to report to work as usual. He assumed nothing ever took place and continued working as usual.

He who laugh last laughs best.

Some months down the line, he saw another advert, this time round from an assurance company. He applied, and through the recommendations of his supervisors, he was able to get the job. The pay was much better compared to the one he had missed months earlier. Later on, my brother learned that political and tribal influence could have contributed to his loss of opportunity in a company that he worked so hard for as an intern and even after graduation.

Our challenge segment.

➢ What do we learn from this story?
➢ What qualities does Peter have?
➢ If you were in his place, what could you have done?
➢ Some people can fail you at the point of your greatest weakness. As an intelligent person, how are you to deal with such frustrations?

Big lesson from the story above.

❖ Always give your best despite the pay.
❖ Never hand in your resignation due to anger.
❖ When one door closes, God will open another for you.
❖ Do not be choosy; first take the job that is available.
❖ Never lose focus of your vision; do not be distracted by life challenges and give up.
❖ Always keep your eyes open for better opportunities.

Chapter Two

THE UNEMPLOYMENT CRISES IN KENYA AND THE GLOBE

What is unemployment rate?

The unemployment rate of a country refers to the share of people who want to work but cannot find jobs. This includes workers who have lost jobs and are searching for new ones, workers whose jobs ended due to an economic downturn, and workers for whom there are no jobs because the labour supply in their industry is larger than the number of jobs available.

Kenya Unemployment Rate From 2008- 2019

Year	Unemployment rate
2019	9.31%
2018	9.31%
2017	9.29%
2016	9.63%
2015	9.68%
2014	9.59%
2013	9.79%
2012	9.66%
2011	9.68%
2010	9.73%
2009	9.6%
2008	9.93%

Unemployment elsewhere in the world.

i. U.S.A., March 2020 - 4.4%
ii. United Kingdom, March 2020 - 5.3%
iii. France, February 2020 - 8.1%
iv. Spain, February 2020 - 13.6%
v. Germany, February 2020 - 3.2%
vi. China, March 2020 - 5.9%

Note.

The unemployment rate in 2020 and beyond is likely to change drastically due to the global pandemic of COVID 19 disease. Therefore, it is wise to consider the figures from March 2020 backwards.

The touching story of Kelvin Ochieng
A problem shared is a problem half solved. (English Proverb)

The story of Kelvin Ochieng is perhaps the most touching when it comes to unemployment. Kelvin sat for his KCPE and scored 392 marks out of a possible 500. This was good performance in Kenyan standards. This earned him an admission at Maranda National School (Kenya) where he continued with his exemplary performance. He outclassed his colleagues and became an index one candidate. When he sat for his KCSE, he managed to score a mean grade of A. straight A's in all the subjects except English which he scored a B+ plus. This achievement earned him a spot at the University of Nairobi, one of the best universities in Kenya. In the university, he specialized in Actuarial Science.

"I was looking forward to a great course that will give me a good job, so I settled for Actuarial Science," said Kelvin. Courtesy of loans from HELB and other sponsorship programs, Kelvin was able to finish his university education. He was able to score **first-class honours.** Unfortunately he never had the opportunity to attend his graduation because of lack of money.

Kelvin's Great Struggles.

These admirable achievements were not so rewarding to Kelvin. Years of handwork with outstanding academic results proved less beneficial until he ended up on the streets of Nairobi, **jobless and homeless.** Searching for either internship opportunities or job became the most difficult thing to find. "The problem of not getting a job comes when I feel that I am qualified but I don't get the job, so I get frustrated and that is how I found myself on the streets., Narrated Kelvin.

Societal Judgement

With an intelligent mind, he lived on the streets for days when it was apparent that his rural home was no better place as his family and the society in general expected too much from him. "It happened that I went home before. People there live in abject poverty. Having gone to the university, I am the star of the family who is expected to get them out of poverty. That belief haunted me because I believed it was my duty to help them. I even contemplated suicide," Kelvin lamented.

Kelvin's Home in the Slum

After days in the cold streets of Nairobi, Kelvin finally found a place to call home when a Good Samaritan, Christopher Oloo came calling. This is how he landed in **Mathare slums.** Said Oloo, "I met him on the streets and he told me that he is a graduate. It sounded hilarious and so strange. I could not believe. When we went to a cyber, it became clear that he had scored clean A's. I was shocked how a graduate could live in the streets?"

Together, Kelvin and his new friend lived for months in Mathare, ekking out a living from menial jobs in the market streets of Nairobi and scrabbling with many uneducated people for car washing jobs.

Kelvin Gets Help

It was only when the story of Kelvin was aired in Citizen Television [Kenya] that Kelvin was offered a job by a company in Kenya. He had struggled and faced all the pains of unemployment. The good thing however, is that it was when he started washing cars that the society realized who he really was. "When he became humble and accepted to wash cars, God uplifted him."

Our challenge segment

➤ Putting yourself in the shoes of Kelvin, what options did he have?
➤ Apart from formal employment that was not forthcoming, what next for "Kelvin?"
➤ What would be your starting point if you ever find yourself in such a situation?

Big lessons from the story above

❖ Good grades is not always a guarantee to formal employment.
❖ We should always prepare for the worst as we hope for the best.
❖ When things get tough, only the tough get going.
❖ If you get a job, do it well, respect it!
❖ In college/university, take time to think about other options to lean on if things do not turn out as expected.

Chapter Three

WHY YOU HAVE AN ADVANTAGE
AS A GRADUATE

According to Saumi Dutta of University of Calcutta, India, getting a job should not be the final destination of education. The sole purpose of education according to Dutta is to purify one's heart, soul and mind and to stand above all the hypocrisies and superstitions. It is to be able to discern facts from speculations, to be morally polite and humble, to be able to introspect into the self and find out the faults and fallacies in character and to build oneself strong enough to bring positive changes in the society for the betterment of human evolution.

Dutta continues to suggest that, "Making money without being educated needs some special skills." Now does this mean that someone without college or university education cannot make it in business? No. History is filled with college dropouts' millionaires. However, statistically, in order to be a higher earner or performer in business, some level of education is recommended.

Your advantage is because, first, you are an educated mind. Secondly, you have acquired the right skills which can guide you in starting a business venture. Formal education gives you an upper hand in entrepreneurship. You are well endowed and equipped with what it takes. You can negotiate for a business deal, communicate effectively, do calculations, market something, and most importantly, organise or reorganise yourself to face the challenges of life courageously. Being a graduate puts on your shoulders the big task of being a problem solver, not only for you but also for your family and state. Why am I saying this? Am alluding to the fact that God has endowed you with a powerful brain and talents to the effect that you can trigger innovations for self fulfilment and progress.

Our main problem as graduates is setting our minds fully on employment. We should always use our education and qualifications to survive if things do not turn out as expected. There is nothing wrong in being employed. In fact, if you are able to secure a job after graduation, the better since your life will be much easier even when it comes to setting up a business venture. However, this ought not to be your ultimate goal. Robin Thomas, Executive Director, Counselling and Psychotherapy put it this way:

> There is a difference between qualification and education. Qualification is merely information, instruction, learning and practice. But education is our circumstances, situations and relationships, interactions, growing up, realisations, emotional awareness and what life in general teaches us. Those who are qualified restrict their careers around their qualifications, but those who are educated and conditioned by life's experiences come out of the box, think on their own, leave aside their ego and do whatever they are forced to do due to circumstances and situations in order to survive.

So as a graduate, use both your qualification and education to come up with something if things go south after your graduation.

Our challenge segment.

➤ Are you educated or qualified?
➤ Have you ever wondered how you can apply your education and qualification in bettering your life and that of the society in general?
➤ What differentiates you from those who never made it in academics?
➤ If you were not educated, how would you survive out there?

Big lessons from the information above.

❖ It is education not your qualification that will take you far.
❖ Educated people are able to do what it takes to survive in difficult situations.
❖ Educated people always come up with a solution.
❖ Educated people have an advantage over the untrained.
❖ Educated people are able to put their ego aside when things go south.

Chapter Four

THE RIGHT PATH: FOLLOWING YOUR PASSION

You have no job, so where do you begin?

Where there is a will there is a way. (English Proverb)
This is a big fat question. For sure, unemployment can do you a number of harm like destroying your self-esteem, not to mention your bank account. If you have been papering the world with resumes and not getting any nibbles, it is easy to sink into frustration, stress and despair. Sad as it is, its a Biblical truth - joblessness if not handled with care can destroy you. However, you can take some small comfort in the knowledge that you are not alone in your struggle to secure a job. To say the least, handwork, ingenuity, and willingness to ask for help are key in getting a job. If you do not ask, you will never find.

The other unfortunate truth is that it is more difficult to get a job when you do not have one. Fair or not, almost all employers often prefer to hire candidates that are currently working or employed. Therefore, if you are doing nothing after graduation, you can be sure that you are standing on a landmine that is likely to crush you into the world of unemployment for a long time. So get up and be useful.

Tips to getting a job

1) Get something to do/ be useful.
You must first look for something to do. For example, you can open an account and start working on online jobs. If you do not get a job online, ask those who have busy online accounts to offer you some work. You can also try your lack as a casual labourer in a factory or firm. If you are in the

rural areas, do some simple agro-business. Engage in family business if there is one. Generally, you have to look for something to do no matter how little the pay is. If you have some cash, make a simple business plan and hit the road. This is very important as it will occupy your mind and save you from drifting into stress and despair.

2) Talk to People.

It is very true that having your ear on the ground can help you find a job. You can get information through networking. What I mean is that you must know how to build and maintain good relationships with your colleagues in college/university. Social networks, having their contacts, being on a Whatsapp group, etc, are important ways to keep in touch with others. If you have a character that can relate well with them, they are very likely to refer you to an opportunity that they may hear of. But if you are those bad boys and nasty girls in college, chances are that even if people hear of a job vacancy, they may not recommend it to you.

The other thing here is that you should let people know that you are searching for a job, including family, friends, relatives, your lecturer or personal tutor, your friends in church and so on. The wider the network search, the better. Do not be embarrassed to ask for help, but also be keen not to nag or beg. Be polite and professional. On the other hand, do not rely on people to get a job for you. They can help, but that is not their responsibility. Do not hold grudges if some fail to help you.

3) Volunteer.

Working with no pay sometimes sounds stupid, but it works for some people. If you do not have a financial backup that can facilitate you during the volunteering period, you cannot manage it. The trick here is gathering information about those organisations that give lunch and transport to their volunteer staff. If you are lucky to get such a chance, go for it. Never volunteer blindly. The benefit of offering voluntary service is that they help in expanding and building your social networks thus making it easier for you to get a job. They also help in enriching your resume.

According to a survey by Deloitte (2016), the vast majority of respondents agreed that volunteering improved a person's leadership and professional skills. There is also data showing that eighty-two per cent of people in the USA involved in hiring decisions, on seeing volunteer work on a candidate's resume, would make them more likely to hire that person. This principle is applicable everywhere in the globe. If you have ever volunteered in a certain company, hospital, hotel etc, you stand a better chance of being hired as compared to those who have never. Another thing is that whether it is voluntary or not, you must always give your best.

4) Explore beyond your country.

If you are a professional, and you have the confidence that you can work anywhere in the world, this could be your chance. The problem here is that nowadays, there is a lot of human trafficking. With Africa and Asian countries being the worst hit. So do a thorough research and apply for a job abroad. Some organisations can even facilitate your ticket fee.

Warning: avoid countries like India, Middle East Nations (with an exception of Israel) and Mexico. India is notorious for sex-trade and sex-slave business. Arab nations are notoriously known for mistreating foreign workers to the extent of killing them. Mexico is the worst nation of all due to drugs related crimes and women being sexually abused. You can still work in those nations but you need to be extremely vigilant especially if you are a woman. Good countries include Israel, USA, UK, China, Canada, Australia, France, Italy and Japan et al. Though they may also have some elements of racism and other prejudices, they are better compared to the former. To increase your chance of survival outside your country, try as much as possible to get connected to a person you know who resides and works there. This person could be your friend, family friend or distance relative.

Note.

Women need to be extra vigilant when travelling abroad, because of the vast human trafficking business going on in the world. Also, make sure you get a work permit when you get into a foreign country.

5) Increase your skill.

Sometimes it may be necessary to add some more skills in your career for you to become employable or fit in certain organisations. This is true because the more diverse your skills are, the better. If you have no money like most graduates, look for certifications or training that you could take, especially the ones that are offered for free by various agencies or at a very low fee. Courses like CPA can be done at home if you can manage to book and pay for exams. There are also various free courses offered by local and international institutions on their online platforms.

6) Brand yourself.

Personal branding refers to the art of packaging yourself for the job market by marketing and positioning your skills and competencies. By branding yourself, you are literally putting yourself as an expert in your field. You are defining how you will appear in the job market. In a non-professional language, everyone has a brand: it is how people think and say about you in your absence. The simplest way of branding yourself is by following the following tips:

a) Identify your talent. What are you good at? What can you do best? What do you enjoy doing? This can also be your passion.

b) Better your best. Practise makes perfect. You have to improve on your weakness. For instance if your weakness is in making presentations, learn from others who are doing it better and perfect it through practice. Perfecting your skills and knowledge through learning and research will go a long way in making you better.

c) Be consistent. You cannot do a great job today and a shoddy one tomorrow. If you are not consistent, people will never value you highly, and sooner or later, you will be forgotten. Your brand must be known, and respected for what it delivers. You cannot afford to fail at any time. Ask yourself questions like, What makes successful brands like Amazon, Safaricom, Equity Bank tick? The answer is simple: consistence in service delivery.

d) Remain relevant. What you are offering should relate to the product or activities of the targeted organisation or firm. For you to remain relevant, you must be open to new ideas and technology. Learn from others and avoid know it all mentality and attitude. If you do not remain relevant, replacement is inevitable. Remember that we are living in a time when organisations are always looking for a person to fire in order to hire someone who is cheaper. Some of the employers will even do something to provoke you to resign, like reducing your salary. Ask yourself, If you handed in your resignation letter today, what would be your boss's reaction? Will they tell you to reconsider it by giving you additional benefits or will they be relieved to have you gone? It all depends on your personal brand.

Note.
If you have a problem branding yourself, or working alone as a brand, you can always look for other jobless graduates, and together, you can work out a plan.

7) Always prepare well for interviews.

One the reason why you could be jobless is because you have a badly written resume or a poor self presentation during the actual interview. Most graduates leave interview rooms thinking, "I am hired." They get a rude shock when they hear that they did not make it through. When it comes to interviews, make sure you put your best foot forward. This means doing everything possible to make sure you have increased your chance of being hired. According to Michael Tomaszewski, CPRW, (Certified Professional Resume Writer) and Career expert, a good CV should meet the following criteria:

a) You should always pic the best CV format. Recruiters spend only six seconds scanning each CV, which means that first impression is very important. If your CV is neat and properly organised, you will convince the recruiters to spend more time on it. This will definitely enhance your chance of being shortlisted for the interview.

b) Always choose clear legible fonts. - Go for the standard CV typefaces: Arial, Tahoma or Helvetica if you prefer sans-serifs fonts and Times New Romans or Bookman Old Style if serif fonts are your pick. Use 11 to 12 font size and single spacing. For your name and section title, pick 14 to 16--font size.

c) Be consistent with your CV layout. Set one-inch margin for all sides. Make sure tour CV headings ate uniform: make them larger and in bold but go easy on italics and underlining. Stick to a single date format throughout your CV.

d) Get photos off your CV. Unless you are explicitly asked to include your photograph in the job ad.

e) Make your CV brief and Relevant. - do not be one of those candidates stuck in the nineties who think they have to include every single detail about their lives on their CV. Write only those details relevant to the job that you are applying for.

f) Add Your Contact information appropriately. You want the recruiters to get back to you, so give them credible contact details. The tricky part is that some recruiters will use your details to know more about you. If your social media accounts are full of rubbish, forget about the job.

g) Start with a CV Personal Profile, CV Summary or CV Objective. After listing their contact information on the CV, most candidates jump right into their work experience and education. So how do you make a CV pop? All it takes is a CV personal profile statement: a short, snappy paragraph of about 100 words that tells the recruiter why you are just the candidate they have been looking for.

- Your personal profile will be either a CV objective or a CV summary.

- A CV objective shows what skills you have mastered and how you would fit in the job. It is a good choice if you have little work experience relevant to the job you are trying to land on.

- A CV summary highlights your career progress and achievements. Use it if you are a seasoned professional and have a lot of experience in your field. Let us look at some examples.

Example of a CV objective

Candidate A

Newly licensed Nurse looking for a challenging nursing role in a medical facility where I can put my skills to the test. WRONG.

Candidate B.
Dependable licensed Registered Nurse, trained to work in high-stress environments with a capacity of staying calm under pressure. Seeking to leverage meticulous record-keeping and analytical skills to help St. Francis Hospital with your upcoming challenges. RIGHT.

Example of a CV Summary.
Candidate A
Bilingual (English and Dutch) paediatric Nurse with fifteen plus years' experience in the intensive and neonatal care unit of a community hospital. Seeking to leverage management experience as chief Paediatric Nurse at General Hospital, helping to implement new staff training programmes. RIGHT.

Candidate B.
Paediatric Nurse with years of experience supervising the medication and health records of new-borns. WRONG.

h) List your relevant work experience and key achievements.
More often than not, your work experience section is the most important part of your whole CV. It is the one that gets the most eye time, so you have to make it attractive and eye-catching. The recruiter wants to know: what you did, how well you did it and what you can offer your prospective employer. Therefore, to make it attarctive, do the following:
  i.   Focus on your measurable, relevant achievements, not just duties.
  ii. Use action verbs e.g. created, analysed, implemented not responsible for creating, analysing and implementating.
  iii. Tailor your CV to the job posting. Read carefully the job description and check what tasks will be expected of you. If you have done them before, put them on your CV, even if they were not your primary responsibilities.

Note.
I would advise you to seek help from an experienced resume writer if you have a problem in the area.

Our challenge segment

➤ Have you ever tried to look for employment/job before? How did it go?
➤ What is your personal brand?
➤ Do you think you already have the right networks that can connect you to places when looking for a job?
➤ What do you do during the long holidays? Have you ever thought of voluntary services?
➤ Do you know people who work outside the country? Have you ever tried to connect with them?
➤ If you graduate today, will you have saved some money to help you get started in life?

Big lessons from the information above

❖ It is important to have or to develop a personal brand.
❖ Good and healthy networking is crucial when seeking for a job.
❖ It is always good to prepare thoroughly for an interview.
❖ Talking to people and voluntary services can help you get a job.
❖ It is possible to explore job opportunities in other countries.

Summary on Job Seeking.

If you have tried all the tricks above and nothing is forth coming, it is time to try something else: Entrepreneurship.

Chapter Five

ENTREPRENEURSHIP
"The true entrepreneur is a doer, not a dreamer." (Nolan Bushnell.)

What is entrepreneurship?
Entrepreneurship refers to the art and science of innovation and risk-taking for profit in business. In a non-professional language, entrepreneurship is the activity of setting up a business or taking on financial risks in the hope of getting profit from it.

So where do you start?
The good thing about entrepreneurship is that you do not have to be a graduate from Cambridge or Harvard school of business to sail through the business world. All you need is to look around what you have. That will be your capital. If you do not have money already, you can sell some of the things that you do not necessarily need, for instance
- ✓ If you have two phones, you can sell one.
- ✓ If you have too many clothes, select some and sell them as second hand.
- ✓ Some electronics can also be sold off in desperate times.
- ✓ You can also borrow money from friends or relatives.
- ✓ If you have domestic animals in your rural home, you can sell them.

The next thing is to establish your passion.
Your passion is that one thing that you have always known you can do with least effort. It is what you always wanted to become. It is what you are made of. When following your passion, you do not need to be taught so much about it or a lot of money to accomplish it. **"Rome was not build in a day."** Gradually is the way to go. The least money you need maybe two thousands or less and the maximum depends on you.

Develop a business plan.

A good business plan guides you through each stage of starting and managing your business. You will use your business plan as a road map for how to structure, run, and grow your new business. Business plans can help you get funding or bring on new business partners. Investors want to feel confident as they want a return on their investments. Your business plan is the tool you will use to convince them that working with you or investing in your business is a smart choice. A simple business plan should at least answer the following five questions.

i. What is the need of your product or service?
ii. What is your competition? How will you distinguish yourself in the market?
iii. How will you make money? E.g. in terms of sales versus expenses.
iv. How will you market your business?
v. How will you get started? I.e. what are your capital requirements?

It should not be a sophisticated one for starters. You only need to research on where to get your items of trade, where you are going to sell them, and how you are likely to make profit. Once you have completed making such plans, it is time to hit the road.

When starting a business, don't use all your capital at once. Always start with small items and let the customers dictate what you are going to add to the stock. This will also give you time to re-evaluate the choice of business and modify it appropriately.

The case of a college graduate in Kibra.
An entrepreneur is someone who jumps off a cliff and builds a plane on the way down. (Reid Hoffman.)

We all know that Kibra is one of the biggest slums in the Kenyan capital, Nairobi. Sometimes back, a teacher, Mr Karanja (not his real name) came to the staffroom with this fascinating story about a young college graduate who had graduated from a renowned college in Kenya with a diploma in catering. Mr Karanja was by then working with an NGO in the area. The NGO wanted to establish ways in which people in the area and especially women and youths could be assisted to come out of poverty. It was then that they came across Ochieng. When Ochieng graduated from college, he spent the first one-year applying for jobs in hotels and schools around Nairobi and beyond. By the end of the year, nothing had come, he had not secured a job. "I did everything, humanly possible to get a job, I remember one day sitting in my room and wondering how I had wasted money going to college." Ochieng narrated.

His life changed one day when he was scrolling down his phone book and came across a peculiar number of a girl who used to be his friend back in college. "It had been two years, and I was very hesitant to make that call, but somehow I gathered some courage, and miraculously someone picked the call." Ochieng continued. "That is the call that changed my life." Ochieng narrated. The girl had already started baking cakes in Kisumu and employed two Boda Boda riders who helped her distribute them around shops and supermarkets in the city. She was planning to open a small baking industry. That was his wake up call.

"For the first time, I felt rreally challenged by that lady. Her questions humiliated me especially when she asked what I was doing. I had to cheat. I told her that I was also baking cakes and selling Chapatis in Kibra and that I own a small restaurant".

The following day, he took a stool, chapati-cooking pan, a roller, bought a 2kg wheat flour packet and started making chapatis along one of the busy Kibra streets. That first day, Ochieng made 200 (two dollars). "It was not a bad start", he said. Later he learned that combining mandazis with chapatis was the trend, so early in the morning, he would prepare mandazis, which he sold in the morning, and chapatis towards lunchtime. Due to his catering skills, his chapatis and mandazis were the best.

Within four months, his earnings had reached Ksh. 1ooo (ten dollars) daily. Two years down the line, his earning had hit Ksh. 2500- 3000 per day, (25-30 dollars) per day. He had also hired a young man to distribute mandazis to kiosks in the area using a bicycle. When Karanja asked him about the initial investment, the response shocked him. "My initial capital was Ksh. 700 (7 dollars.)" When asked if he would consider employment, the answer was obvious, "For now, am enjoying being my own boss and

I have a dream that one day I will own a big hotel". As Karanja and his colleagues concluded the interview, they learned that Ochieng had already bought a plot in Ruai and was in a process of building a three-bedroomed house. Customers were trickling in by around 1 pm, and they had to leave the young man to serve his customers.

Our challenge segment.

➤ If you were to start a business today, which one would, you start?
➤ What will it take you to succeed in that business?
➤ Have you ever thought of having a business plan?
➤ What are your options if you do not have capital?
➤ What lessons do you learn from Ochieng's success?
➤ Ochieng is not a business student yet he seems to sail through in the world of business. What do you think is his big secret?
➤ What do we learn by, "Rome was not build in a day" in business matters?

Big Lessons from the information above.

❖ If you cannot secure a job, you can create your own.
❖ You do not necessarily require big capital to get started.
❖ Learn to grow slowly but consistently.
❖ A business plan can help you get funds for investment.
❖ You can succeed anywhere, including in the slums.
❖ When challenged by the success of your friends, take it positively.

THE POWER OF
STARTING SMALL

You do not need big cash, what you need is a big idea. (N. Michael)
Some people today still cling to the 19th century notion that for you to succeed in business, you must have a lot of money. Most of us do not even care to look at how the journey of some of the successful business ventures has been. We do not care to look at the sacrifices and struggles that some people had to endure to become who they are today. We always conclude in a very ignorant manner: "Those guys are lucky." We do not seek to know the details of their pain, frustrations, their greatest mistakes et al, and ask how those struggles shaped their business models.

The inspiring story of S. K. Macharia, owner of Royal Media Services
Small beginnings are the launching pad to great endings. (Joyce Meyer)
Dr. S. K. Macharia once opened up about his humble beginnings in life as a student in the United States. He was speaking during a prize-giving ceremony at Kahuhia Girls High School in Murang'a sometimes back. The billionaire businessperson said he moved to the US in 1962 to study after winning the Kennedy Airlifts Scholarship.

Who is S.K. Macharia?
Samuel Kamau Macharia (born 1942) is the Kenyan founder and chair of Royal Media Services, the largest private radio and television network in Eastern Africa. In 2012, he was on Forbes magazine's top 10 list by of African millionaires to watch. He was in the 2013 Africa Report of the 50 most influential Africans. He was honoured with the 2015 Eastern

Africa Ernst and Young Entrepreneur Lifetime Achievement Award.

Early life

Macharia was born in Ndakaini Village, Murang'a County in 1942. He has three sisters and is the second born. His parents were squatters in Subukia where they worked in British settler plantations under the colonial government. Macharia's mother died when he was only five. The family moved to Arusha in Tanzania, but his father's attempts at securing employment were unsuccessful. Meanwhile the young Macharia kept the company of Maasai herds boys. He would traverse long distances with them in search of pasture.

Education.

Macharia joined Standard 1 in 1954 at Ndakaini Primary School. Thereafter he was admitted to Gituru Intermediate School, where he sat for the Kenya African Preliminary Examination (KAPE) in 1958. He taught as an untrained primary school teacher at Makomboki Primary School for a year, before joining Kahuhia Teachers Training College. A two-year course at the college would see him qualify as a trained teacher (P3) after which he was subsequently posted to Gituru Primary School in 1961.

He later applied for the Kennedy Airlifts scholarship. He was accepted in the 1962 group. His family could not, however, raise the 4,000 shillings required for the plane ticket to the United States. He could only raise 1,200 shillings and had to travel for nearly two months by road from Kenya to Benghazi, Libya, where he took a ship to England and then a flight to the USA. On arrival, he enrolled in Seattle Technical College and completed his high school education two years later. Macharia would later earn a Bachelor of Arts degree in Political Science from Seattle, Pacific University and a Bachelor of Science degree in Accounting from the University of Washington. He would then complete a Masters of Science degree in Accounting/Finance, a Master of Arts degree in Accounting. He was certified as a Certified Public Accountant (CPA).

Life as a student in USA.

Macharia recounted how for eight years, he worked part-time as a sweeper at the giant Aircraft Manufacturer, Boeing in order to raise his college tuition fees.

"When I was in the US, I worked at night and went to school during the day. Do you know a company called Boeing that makes big planes in Seattle? I swept their floors for eight years. I paid my school fees by working at night and going to school during the day, so there's nothing that you cannot achieve. You don't have to be assisted by anybody but if you get assistance, it's just a small push. It's all about what you are doing for yourself that will make you a person and you will be proud of yourself," he said.

Macharia owns Royal Media Services, which operates TV stations and more than 10 FM stations in Kenya. He also has big investments in real estate and in the hospitality industry.

Lesson from S.K. Macharia's Story.

Reading the story of S.K. Macharia can help us conclude that each one of us is allocated 24 hours a day. It is upon us to decide when to work and when to sleep, how many hours to engage in income generating projects and how many hours to idle. Despite the fact that our talents are not equal, each person has the responsibility of developing and enhancing whatever he/she has for the benefit of self and others.

What does the Bible say about lack of investing mentality?

The parable of the Talents. [Matthew 25:14-30]

In this parable, the master goes away on a trip. Before he leaves, he calls his three servants and entrusts each of them with some money. To one servant, the master gives five thousand gold coins, to the second, two thousand gold coins, and to the third, one thousand gold coins. The first two servants invest their money and double their profits. When the master returns, after a long time, the first two servants give back to their master the original investment plus the profit. The third servant, however, does not invest what he was given by his master but instead buries it in a field. When the master returns, the lazy servant only returns his talent. The master is pleased with the first two servants, but to the third, he is dissatisfied. He reprimands him and casts him out into darkness. The amazing thing is that **the master entrusted those who had taken risk to invest their talents with more.** To the one who did not invest, his only talent was taken away from him and given to the one who brought in much. Jesus concluded the parable thus:

> For to every person who has something, even more will be given, and he will have more than enough; but the person who has nothing, even the little that he has will be taken away from him.

Verse 30 makes it even more interesting:

> As for this useless servant- throw him outside in the darkness; there he will cry and grid his teeth."

In this awesome parable, Jesus teaches his disciples that they are to use their talents, i.e. abilities, skills, intelligence and gifts to serve God without reservation and fear of taking risks. They are to add more people as "profit" into the Kingdom of God. The master also expects the one who has more talents to bring in more profit, but is not happy about the servant who is afraid of taking risks. God has commanded us **to work.** In fact the bible is very clear that, **"if you don't work, you should not eat."** How then do we work? God has given us talents in different measures. He expects us to use our talents; intelligence, education, skills, gifts et al to profit for own good and for the good of His kingdom.

My brother- in-law Humble Beginnings.
"Big things have small beginnings." (Michael Fassbinder.)

After graduating from technical college and applying for jobs in several firms, my brother-in-law could not secure formal employment. He had not even saved anything substantial. Finally, a certain rich man in his neighbourhood was building an apartment in Githurai, Nairobi. My brother in-law, Kuria (not his real name) applied for the job together with other young men from the village. Luckily, the rich man recognised Kuria since they attended the same Catholic Church, which earned him a place as a supervisor of the whole project. For two years, Kuria had earned a lot to the extent of buying a second hand Nissan Matatu. Kuria had always dreamed of owning a Matatu. Since the project was still going on, he employed his elder brother as the driver of his Matatu as he continued working for the rich neighbour. They had agreed that his brother was to deposit Ksh.3000 each day in Kuria's bank account. For the first four months, Kuria would rush to the bank to check his balance. Everything seemed fine, so he stopped checking and hoped that his brother would keep his word. After about a year and three months, the project ended and the rich man thanked Kuria for a job well done.

Kuria's Greatest Shock

On returning home, Kuria encountered the shock of his life. His Matatu placed on stones near his compound. At first, it did not look like the Matatu he had spent all his fortune to buy, but looking closely at the number plate, the truth hit him like a bomb. His brother, on phone, explained that he abandoned the car after it developed some mechanical problems. "That car was bad, you should thank God that it did not cause an accident." To make the matters worse, Kuria was almost becoming a father. He had met and married a girl in Githurai. It was double tragedy. The following day, he called a mechanic who asked for twenty five thousand to fix it to roadworthiness.

With the family responsibility at hand, Kuria had to think fast. He had no such money, but his account had some twenty thousand which he used to repair the matatu. He started looking for someone to buy it. Being out of shape, it would not fetch much. When someone offered him Ksh. 100,000, he took it, out of frustration and lack of capacity to repair it further. He had bought it at Ksh. 200,000. Kuria bought a motor cycle for Ksh 75, 000. This enabled him to start operating a Boda Boda business. He was back to square one.

Kuria Break-Through

In 2014, Kuria went to Mombasa and took a New Toyota Nissan Matatu on loan. I remember the last time I was in his place, he was operating three Boda Bodas. In 2019, he had managed to complete paying the loan. He was now planning to sell his Toyota Box matatu and get a Mini-Bus in 2020. I pray that God will help him accomplish his dream.

Our challenge Segment

➤ Whom would you identify with among the three servants in the parable of the talents?

➤ If you have been given more, a lot is expected of you. Do you believe in this assertion?

➤ Some people are always afraid of taking risks. What lessons do they learn from the parable of the talents?

➤ When we trust people with our money and then they fail us, what should we do? Do we abandon our vision because of such misfortunes?

➤ What motivates Kuria?

➤ Having read about Kuria, do you think he will succeed in his quest of buying a Mini-Bus Matatu?

➤ Hard work pays. How do you relate this to the early struggles of S.K. Macharia?

Big Lessons from the Illustrations Above

❖ You do not need a lot of capital to start a business.

❖ Always be ready to take calculated risks.

❖ Do not be too eager to trust people with your investments.

❖ If you lose your investment, start all over again.

❖ God does not rewards cowards who are never willing to try anything.

❖ Your passion can propel you to start something, but it's your persistence and commitment that will make you successful.

❖ Handwork is rewarded.

❖ Education empowers you to chase your dreams, not employment.

Chapter 7

VENTURE IN A
BUSINESS YOU UNDERSTAND

Better, the Devil you know. (English Proverb)

One good thing I know about investment is that it helps people achieve other financial goals that they could have otherwise not achieved. Personally, I do not buy the idea that young people need a financial advisor. "For what?" What they need is basic financial education. Relatively speaking, some young starters can't afford such services. My advise therefore to young starters: first engage in business areas or fields that you know how to run. This does not mean that you have to be a paragon in that field. No, but what I am putting across is the fact that you cannot succeed in a business venture if you do not know how it goes. You need information on how things flow from the source to the market and the dynamics involved in every step. Failure to do so is like stepping on hot coal. You will not withstand it.

Mr Njenga and His Matatu Business

Mr Njenga (not his real name) left university in the 90s when being a graduate was taken very seriously and, by luck, was posted to a school by the Teacher Service Commission (TSC) immediately. He never experienced what we call tarmacking. Young and with a payslip. He is a maths and physics teacher, so when it comes to calculating profits, loss and other nitty grittys, he is top-notch. Through a friend, Njenga was introduced to the matatu business. He did some mental calculations, as most mathematics paragons do and concluded, "I am in." Those days, KCB bank was for "the high class citizens" and Equity was still having teething problems. He approached the bank and borrowed a loan. Within no time, he had a Matatu operating between Wangige, Kawangware and the big city Nairobi. For the first few months, it was "A dream come true opportunity."

The money was so good that to some extent, Njenga contemplated dumping TSC for its "peanuts." He was ready to join the likes of Njenga Kurume, John Harun Mwau, Pius Ngugi and Adil Popat among other s who were not only smelling money but making a real kill those days. However, the situation would soon take a turn. The matatu business soon put his skills in Maths and Physics to a test. It was about the eighth month that he started noticing whimsical behaviours from his employees.

"They started by bringing less money and complaining that the day was bad. Police cases became so numerous, and the vehicle started having endless mechanical problems", He narrated to me. "Whenever I succeeded in solving one problem another one cropped up. I started changing drivers and conductors, but after a few months, the problem would recur. Sometimes they would call me in the middle of a lesson. I would excuse myself to go and find out what was happening, only to discover that they were cheating. It was so frustrating. I started having problems with my wife back at home because most of the times, I would go home very angry after a bitter exchange with the driver, conductor or both. Sometimes, I could sleep without eating, hungry and angry." Njenga concluded.

Njenga is forced to quit
Better, lose the saddle than the horse. (Proverb)

Later Njenga had to quit. Things were moving from bad to worse. For a moment, he was flying, but tables turned, and he was now crashing. His relationship with his wife worsened by the day. Therefore, to save his marriage and his venture, he decided to sell the matatu. He took the money and completed paying the KCB loan. In other words, it was like starting from zero. Everything stopped. The Matatu business was over, but Njenga and his family were now "free from stress."

Our challenge segment

➤ What is Njenga's main problem?

➤ Did Njenga take time to understand the Matatu Business?

➤ What was Njenga biggest opportunity and how did he spoil it?

➤ Njenga lost the business but gained a lesson. Was it worth it?

➤ How relevant is the saying, "Better the Devil you know" in Njenga's story?

➤ Njenga and Family were now "free from stress." How peculiar is this statement?

Great lessons from the illustration above

❖ Always take time to understand a business before making an investment in it.

❖ When the risk is high and the boat is sinking, walk out before everything comes down crashing.

❖ Avoid moving with the crowds but understand your niche.

❖ Bad business decisions lead to bad results.

❖ Successful matatu business requires a hands-on approach. It is not easy for someone who is tied up in an office job from 8 am to 5pm to run it smoothly. Do you agree on this?

❖ It is always advisable to have a GPS tracker on your Matatu so that you can monitor the number of trips it makes during the day and its location all the time.

Chapter Eight

THE POWER OF
INNOVATION

A good mind possesses a kingdom (English Proverb.)

The Societal perspective of innovation.

Innovation by definition is the introduction of something new. Without innovation, there is not anything new and without anything new, there will be no progress. If an organisation is not making any progress, it simply cannot stay relevant in the competitive market.

Innovation is undoubtedly the core reason for modern existence. Change is inevitable, and in most cases, innovation creates positive change. Technological innovation is considered a major source of economic growth. Economic growth refers to the increase in the inflation-adjusted market value of goods and services produced by an economy over time. It is conventionally measured as the percent rate of increase in real gross domestic product (GDP). Essentially, there are two ways to increase the output of the economy:

i. Increase the number of inputs that go to the productive process.
ii. Come up with new ways to get more output from the same number of inputs.

The latter describes the essence of innovation quite well. The purpose of innovation is to come up with new ideas and technology that increase productivity and generates greater output with the same input. Technological advancement and increased productivity means a major change in careers as well. The world economy could more than double by 2050 due to continued improvement in technology-driven products. According to the New World Economic Forum report, nearly 133 million new jobs may be created by 2022 while 75 million jobs are likely to be displaced by automation and robotics. Generally, innovation and economic growth improves living standards. According to the Brooking

Institution in Washington D.C., USA, the average life satisfaction is higher in countries with greater GDP per capita. Another research also shows that there is a link between innovation and subjective well-being.

Developing countries depend on innovation as new digital technologies and innovative solutions create huge opportunities for fighting sickness, poverty, unemployment, and hunger. Developed nations also rely on innovation to be able to solve their own problems related to these themes.

How to go about Innovation
Innovation distinguishes between a leader and a follower. (Steve Jobs)

Six Steps towards Innovative Ideas

1) Document your plan/vision.
Everyone has ideas on how he/she can make it in life, but the reality is that most people never take time to sit down and give their vision/dream/plan time to sink in their mind. The risk has always been that if the ideas are not put in writing, chances of being acted upon or being realized are very remote. If the ideas are not put in writing, they face the risk of:
a) Becoming distorted.
b) Evaporation.
c) Becoming irrelevant or outdated.

To some extent, if an idea is not put down in writing, you are likely to start questioning its viability or your capacity to realize it. If on the other hand, it is written down, the opposite happens and you start having a more clearer view on how such an idea can be accomplished. So, always start by writing down your idea or vision.

2) Identify a problem that requires your solution.
Here, you need to find out whether your innovation is about a problem worth solving in the society. What gaps will your innovation fill? This is very important since innovations are for finding better and easier ways of doing things. If the problem is worth solving, it should adequately answer the following questions:
a) Are my products/services something that customers need/must

have?

b) Are my products/services affordable or will the customers pay for them?

c) Are there other products/services in the market offering the same? What makes my products/services better?

d) How feasible is my plan/project in the current market trend?

e) If you are satisfied that your product is feasible and that it can address the problem and more so people will be willing to pay for it, then you can go on with your plan.

3) Share with your friend.

Indirectly share your innovative ideas with your friends. You can put it across in the following ways:

a) I read a book and there was this idea on ….what do you think about it?

b) I watched a movie and there was a great idea about… what do you think about it?

c) My business teacher used to suggest that… do you think it is practical.

Without realizing it, people will be giving worthwhile comments about your innovative ideas. Some of the ideas will be positive while others are likely to be negative. You will therefore be able to measure how the common people would take it which will inform you on how to deliver or package your innovation. Be careful not to disclose so much as there are many people there who are good at watering down such thoughts.

4) Identify the Risks involved.

Building a successful product is fundamentally about risk mitigation. Therefore, in your innovation plan, you must identify the challenges or limitations of your product and the risks involved if you invest your time and money in the project. Focus here should be creating a product with great efficiency within your means without compromising on its quality. This means that you have to sit down and plan meticulously on how the risk will be minimised. Remember, time wasted is money lost.

5) Test the Market.

Here you have to take your product or innovation to the market. If for instance you are dealing with manufacturing, you need to manufacture a few items and see how the market will handle them. You can do this by:

a) Offering a few products for free as long as the recipient agrees on giving an honest feedback.
b) Running a simple promotion for the product in a target market.
c) Offering discounts for the buyers who buy a certain quantity.

Market testing helps you in identifying the strength and /or weakness of your product or service. It also gives you the most important thing: feedback. Once you have the necessary feedback, it is time to act appropriately to ensure you meet the customers' needs.

6) Launch and grow systematically.

Launching a new product should be done carefully to avoid incurring huge loses. The launch should first target a specific market before engaging in wide scale expansions. This is because the small market or zone (A) acts as a learning ground for the manufacturer, or the innovator. The lessons learned in zone (A) helps in improving the product or the service before venturing into zone (B) and into other market zones. It is extremely risky to have a big launch since in case of a problem in the product, the innovator is forced to re-call all the products in the market, something that will make him/her incur huge loses. During this stage, it is very important that you take customer feedback seriously, since these few customers form the root of a huge customer base in the end.

The growth of a company or brand should take the model of a growing child. It should not run before walking or stand before crawling. This is because all these steps build on each other until the company gains a multinational status.

Innovation in business
Change calls for innovation, and innovation leads to progress (Li Keqiang)

It is difficult to identify industries where innovation is unnecessary. Although certain industries depend on innovation more than others, innovation and the ability to improve considers everyone. It is key to realize that even in highly regulated industries such as taxis and banks, innovation is key in their daily operations. Uber for instance has brought critical changes in how the taxi business is run globally. In general, innovation can deliver significant benefits and is one of the critical skills for achieving success in any business.

According to Steven Johnson in *The Business of Innovation,* innovation does not come just by giving people incentives: it comes from creating environments where their ideas can connect. This, unfortunately, is not so for many African countries which explains why Africa still lags behind when in innovative technological advancement as compared to countries like China.

Is innovation good for Business?
Case Study - Safaricom Limited (Kenya)

The M-Pesa Story. (Kenya)

Safaricom can be described as the African Giant of Innovation when it comes to telecommunication services. In 2007 it launched a mobile phone based money transfer service called M- Pesa. Due to its success in Kenya, the service has since been expanded to Tanzania, Mozambique, DRC, Lesotho, Ghana, Egypt, Afghanistan, South Africa, India, Romania and Albania.

The great thing about M-pesa is that it allows one to do almost all financial transactions with their phones: you can deposit, withdraw, transfer, buy credit, pay for goods and services, access credit and savings, etc. To make it even more interesting, Safaricom has recently introduced another feature in their M-pesa that allows users to complete their M-pesa transactions even when they do not have sufficient funds in their account, called **Fuliza.** Due to these innovative nature of the company, it has always beaten its competitors when it comes to profit margins. Recently, the company declared a net profit of **Ksh 74.7 billion** for the year ending

March 31st 2020, representing a **19.5%** growth in earnings from 2019. The Company attributed its growth to M-pesa and data respectively. |bout innovation, Safaricom says, *"Innovation is central to achieving our strategic objectives, retaining our competitive edge and ensuring that we continue to grow."*

What about individual innovations?

The innovation Story of Roy Allela (Kenya)

Inspired by his great urge to communicate with his 6-year-old niece who was born deaf, Roy Allela, a 25-year-old Kenyan techpreneur **invented Sign-10, a pair of smart gloves with flex sensors to aid his cousin's communication with the other members of the family.** The flex sensor is stitched to each finger, aids in quantifying the letters formed from the curve of each finger of the glove's wearer. The gloves are then connected through Bluetooth to a mobile phone application that vocalizes the hand movements. "My niece wears the gloves, pairs them to her phone or mine, then starts singing, and I'm able to understand what she's saying," Allela stated.

The application also takes into account speed, language, gender and the pitch of the vocals, putting into account that different people have different needs. The gloves can also be customized into the client's specification and style, which Allela explained aims to fight the stigmatization that comes with being deaf. His commitment to making this innovation a success translates to an accuracy result of 93%, making him the winner of the prestigious **Trailblazer Award by the American Society of Mechanical Engineers.**

The Innovation Story of Vitalis Kiplagat. (Kenya)
A multipurpose candle that gives light, fights mosquitos and provide a pleasant smell in the house.

A young man, Vitalis Kiplagat living in Wanye area, Nairobi has rocked the science world by inventing a herbal candle which fights off mosquitoes and other breeding insects common in residential homes.

The bright mind shared the events leading to this intriguing invention giving credit to a high school clean up event.

"We were in school burning rubbish that had the leaves of some plant and I noticed that the bees hiding in the nearby bushes flew away after they came into contact with smoke from the fire. That is when I got interested in finding out why they flew away," Kiplagat recounted. His tools consist of a gas cooker, test tubes, solid wax, beakers, a pestle and motor set and a string used in the candle. The active ingredients of the candle are from the locally available *lantana camara* and blue gum tree leaves that he grinds in the pestle and mortar. On the other side, he boils wax in a beaker until it liquefies.

"One of these two leaves is anti-microbial meaning it prevents breeding of any insect in the house. If you light this candle in your house, all the insects will flee," Kiplagat explained. Once he is done with the grinding, he adds a solvent into the groud powder, which forms a green solution. He dips the string into the solution. The string is then put in the boiling wax solution to harden it. The carefully crafted herbal solution is then added to the boiling wax and the entire solution poured in small portions into the test tubes that already have the pieces of the hardened string cut to fit the size of the test tube. The test tubes with the green solution of the groud leaves and wax are cooled in water until the entire solution solidifies. These tubes are finally heated over steady fire to pop out of the candles due to accumulating pressure during the heating.

Kiplagat stated that he makes up to 100 candles per day and sells each at Ksh 50/-. This amounts to Ksh. 5000 per day, which is not bad for a starter. He urges young innovators not to get discouraged, but to push on until they get results. He is currently working with Kenya Medical Research Institute (KEMRI) to improve on his craft and come up with more by-products from his invention.

We are going nowhere without innovation
Exploration is the engine that drives innovation. Innovation drives economic growth. (Edith Widder.)
For a country like Kenya to create jobs and become industrialised as per

Vision 2030, innovation is necessary. The youths who are leaving colleges and universities must be aware of the fact that without innovative minds, very few or no new jobs opportunities will be available. Innovation is the driver of development and new opportunities. Without it, our Vision 2030 is just going to be a pipe dream.

According to Valeri Souchkov, a Systematic Innovation Expert, innovation is important since it helps to build and implement new solutions to all kinds of problems, which may not be solved by traditional means, when existing solutions do not help to achieve the desired results. According to him, all progress of human civilisation is based on innovative solutions which eliminate tough problems, resolve conflicts and create new opportunities in every area of human activities: technology, business, health, education, agriculture and social institutions. In Kenya, for instance, if we have to achieve our Vision 2030 Dream, **each of our forty-seven counties must come up with at least one manufacturing industry before the end of year 2025.** This will translate to forty-seven industries translating to more employment opportunities for Kenyans. The industries are supposed to be from what the county produces from their innovations not forgetting assembling industries. This will also help in curbing rural to urban migration, something that has strained cities like Nairobi and Mombasa. This means that each county must establish **Industrial Zones** where production or manufacturing is done both for local consumption as well as for export within Africa and beyond. If that is adopted, massive expansions of road and railway networks should be commensurate with he locations of the industrial zones.

Our challenge segment

➤ College and university students are been called upon to be innovative in order to solve the global challenges of unemployment. How can you implement this at a personal level?
➤ Without innovation, our Vision 2030 is just a pipe dream. How do you respond to such assertions?
➤ A good mind possesses a kingdom. How does this proverb apply in

your personal life as a graduate?
- ➤ Innovative ideas solve almost of our human challenges. Which of these challenges have you personally solved through innovative ideas as a graduate?
- ➤ What do you learn from the innovative story of Kiplagat?

Our Big Lessons from illustrations above
- ❖ There is no real progress without innovative ideas.
- ❖ Innovation is going to help solve the problem of unemployment.
- ❖ Our vision 2030 is unlikely to be achieved if we ignore innovation.
- ❖ Innovation helps in solving personal and societal problems.
- ❖ If each of our 47 counties develop industrial zones and accept innovation, Vision 2030 will become a reality.
- ❖ Expansion of roads and railway networks should be commensurate with our industrialization and other development factors.

Chapter Nine

THE MAGIC POWER OF
CHAMA/SELF-HELP GROUPS

Unity is Strength. (English Proverb)

"Chama", the Swahili word for group refers to informal self-help groups where members contribute an agreed monthly sum of money with the aim of helping each other grow economically. Since their inceptions in the early 1980s due to high inflation rates and unemployment in Kenya, Chamas have tremendously grown to become microfinance savings and loans institution s that enable members to escape the bureaucracy of banks, whilst forming strong community ties.

How do Chamas start?

A Chamas is usually formed by a group of people from the same social class, same profession, work mates or any group of people who agree to work together in order to support each other financially by pulling resources together. Mostly, members of a Chama share the same geographical location. The most important things in a Chama are **trust and loyalty.** A thorough analysis of a person's character is carried out before they are allowed to join. Chamas operate within set rules and guidelines set by members. There are fines and penalties for those who fail to fulfil the laid down obligations. Currently there are even legal agreements between members as these groups are growing tremendously with vast wealth and resources. There are four common Chama structures in Kenya that includes Merry-go-round, Pooled investment Chama, Agriculture Cooperatives and Small-scale Chama Companies.

a)   Merry-go-round Chama.

This is where each member contributes a fixed amount of money per a fixed time. During each Chama meeting, the funds are collected and the whole collection given to a member or two on a rotational basis. Members usually pick numbers which determine their turn of getting the funds, commonly referred to as " eating".

b)   Pooled Investment Chamas.

These Chamas work by each member making a monthly contribution of a certain agreed amount. Apart from this, the members also make some savings using the Chama's account. In case a member need a loan, he/she is given the loan based on his/her savings. The members always act as guarantors in such a case. The monthly contributions made by each member is used to do projects as agreed by the members, for instance, land buying, buying of stocks, bonds, housing et al. If members' contributions is not sufficient,   a loan from a financial institution is taken.

c)   Agricultural Cooperatives (Chamas.)

This is whereby farmers come together to create a large-scale cooperative society to deal with marketing of their farm produce. The farmers then sit down and elect directors to run the society on their behalf based on set rules and regulations. The profit that is made by such a society is shared to the members based on the amount of farm produce they have supplied to the society.

d)   Small-scale Chama Companies.

Members come together and register a company after which they pool resources together for a number of years, say 2-3 years. After accumulating a certain targeted sum of money, a project to undertake is agreed on. Mostly members acquire properties through bank loans. After getting the property, they continue making their monthly contributions to service the loan. Selected directors who act as signatories of the Chama bank account make most of the transactions on behalf of the members. There are rules and regulations set on how the money is used.

The Benefits of Chamas

*"The mind that does not think of investing is a
mind of a poor person."(N. Michael)*

The problem among Kenyan and African youth in general, is thinking that chamas are for the old folks. This misconception is hindering them from investing in big projects. The other problem is that our youths are afraid of taking responsibilities for their financial well-being. Most of them waste their hard-earned money in stupid betting, beer parties and second hand vehicles from China and Japan. This means that even after working for five to ten years as either self-employed or in formal employment, they have nothing tangible to show for it. This carefree lifestyle is what has led to the emergence of a large group of people above 65 years living in abject poverty in Africa. In Kenya, for example the government has been forced to come up with a fund to cater for the aged who have no income at all.

In case the carefree people lose employment, they have nothing to lean on. Therefore, they fall back to abject poverty. Lack of investment when someone is working is what I mostly call a **lack of financial intelligence.** It does not matter how much a person is earning, but if they join a good and serious Chama, they can gather capital to start a serious venture or acquire some properties. Some people observe that poverty is in the mind of the possessor, but for me, **"A mind that does not think of investing is the mind of a poor person."** Chamas have numerous benefits that include:

i.   Economic Independence.

Chamas help their members get loans from banks and other financial institutions easily. This enables the members to expand their business ventures thus becoming more economically stable and independent.

ii.   Retirement Security.

Most people especially those not in formal employment, have problems when they reach retirement age. This is because they have no retirement benefits or pension to depend on in their sunset years. Chamas help such people acquire properties, through the secret of pooling resources together. These properties like farms, plots etc. are then developed to earn a living in old age.

iii.   Discipline in Finances.

Chamas make people develop the habit of saving. The commitment, trust and loyalty demanded by the Chama cultivates a culture of financial discipline in an individual. People always put their Chama money aside before budgeting for anything else. This trend when repeated for many years becomes the norm to these people to the extent that some cannot function without a Chama. Financial discipline is the antidote to poverty.

iv. Creating wealth.

Chamas help people to save for capital to start businesses and expand the existing ones. They also help people to acquire properties that they could not have acquired by working alone. All these factors help these people to create wealth.

v. Challenging Gender and literacy Stereotypes.

Chamas, especially those in rural areas empower women from all status, including those who never stepped a foot in school, thus overcoming gender and literacy stereotypes. Chamas also support women innovations towards making immense economic contributions in their families and the nation at large.

vi. Community Bonding.

Chamas also act as a social space for members to interact and live peacefully within a community set up. They also offer support systems, provide financial guidance, family counselling and advice, and a great space for networking for members' businesses. Some community-based projects can also be organised through Chamas.

vii. Loan without Interest.

One of the most romantic thing about Chama especially Merry-go-round is the fact that people get money interest free. Once it is your time to **"eat"**, no one tells you that you have to repay it with some interest. The contributions for chamas are usually affordable to the members, so even after "eating", continuing with the Chama is easy. You also do not feel cheated, like the way you would usually feel after taking a bank loan knowing that the bank is benefitting from your interests.

The Success Story of Milele Alliance

If ever there were a poster child for sound investment, Milele Alliance would be it. The eight-member investment company — started with 10 members in November 2007 — has an investment portfolio worth KSh35 million. Rose Mbanya, a director of Milele, shared its history.

The 10 member founders of the group came from diverse backgrounds, on a who-knows-who basis. It mattered not their age or professions. What mattered was their shared goal: To collect their resources to achieve financial independence. For eight months, the group met every third Saturday of the month, with the agenda to align its members' synergies and to lay its foundation. They contributed a minimum of Sh30, 000 every month. They also agreed on objectives, rules, a constitution, its banking, accounting and auditing partner, and its legal adviser. Members committed to the group's mandate by signing it.

In August 2008, the group registered Milele Alliance as a limited liability company. The money collected thus far became its share capital. Its first investment was the purchase of two parcels of land — 1.25 acres in Juja and two acres in Elementaita. Member contributions were sufficient to finance the investment. To date, the land has been held in its books for speculative and collateral purposes.

Next, and in line with its five-year strategic plan, Milele focused its resources on an income-generating activity: The purchase and letting of residential property in Thika and Mlolongo. The finances came through member contributions and a mortgage from their banking partner. So far, the mortgage has a small balance remaining. The second five-year plan started in August 2013. It has focused on a car-cleaning service located in Mountain View. A manager on site oversees its operations. Milele's plan is to automate the service. To spread its risk, Milele has also invested in the stock market. So what factors have contributed to Milele's longevity and financial success?

"First, we engage professional services. Accountants and auditors maintain our books. In addition, before we make any investment, our lawyers conduct due diligence. Professionals also give us an objective opinion of the state of our affairs," says Rose. Milele has also employed a full-time investment manager for its portfolio. Second, Milele's rules are clear on how to handle matters. "The two members who exited the group in August 2012 left without acrimony. Accurate records allowed us to settle their entitlement, plus extra." Rose illustrates. These Milele rules also explain why the group has escaped the pitfalls that many a women's group fall into, like personal conflicts and whimsical decision-making.

Lastly, Milele does not view itself as a Chama. Milele views itself as an investment company. Planning for the next five-year investment cycle is underway, a process the group takes seriously.

"The investment company has taught us a lot about having a powerful vision and being confident to execute it in a professional manner while working with and learning from the right professionals. At a personal level, we have bonded as investors and enjoyed seeing our company grow from strength to strength. More importantly, we have remained friends and can still challenge each other in the best interest of the company. Milele is something we are proud to have built," Rose says.

The Mapato Group Story

Mapato Group has defied the challenges of its size to make substantial financial strides. So, where did this group of 17 women begin?

"The idea for a Chama was first conceived as a merry-go-round by six women in our social circles, says Janet, a board member who declined to have her identity revealed. After four months, the women realized that the merry-go-round was not working for them. They decided to recruit friends — working women in their 30s – to join as members. The idea was to pool their resources and invest. The group of 20 members, three of whom live in the diaspora, congregated for its first meeting in March 2010 and registered with the Ministry of Gender, Children and Social Services as a women's group.

As it considered its investment options, Mapato elected its office bearers, documented its constitution, and started making monthly contributions of Sh5, 000 (later upped to Sh7, 500) and an annual subscription of Sh2, 000. Its monthly meetings involved team-building activities for members to bond and talks from investment professionals and managers for inspiration and to educate them on investments and internal management structures. Mapato's first investment was the money market fund in July 2011. Later that year, the group purchased shares in the Kenya Association of Investment Groups, through its Amalgamated Chama Limited. In November 2012, the group purchased four acres of land in Kangundo. Its last investment was the purchase of shares in Safaricom Sacco, in July 2013. The group's total investment currently stands at Sh4 Million. Mapato's progress was steady... until the challenges it is now battling put a pause to it. What are some of these challenges?

According to Janet, its size is a huge obstacle. "We started with 20 members. Early on, the professionals we invited to speak warned us our number was unmanageable, that members would fall off the wagon as we progressed. That happened." The group started to shrink when some members failed to make their monthly contributions on time or to make them at all. Having a constitution in place and a valuation of shares worked in the group's favour as it was clear on how exiting members would transfer their shares. Three members exited the group without severing ties.

Other members failed to participate in-group responsibilities like bookkeeping and administrative duties. Janet says such inactive members were elected into the positions to spur their participation. Sometimes this spurring worked while at other times it did not. Divergent views on how to finance its investments also challenged the group. Most of the members voted against bank loans, others supported Sacco loans. Capital calls were made to boost the cash reserves. Not all members welcomed this decision, however — some thought the calls were on a very short notice while others felt it as too great a financial strain. Yet some members gave way above the set minimum.

Due to these challenges, Mapato has been dormant since December 2013. Janet says that the group will meet again to deliberate on what to do next. She is hopeful that not everything is lost. She says, "This is a fantastic group of women, focused and committed to what they are doing." Given its success in the past three years, it is almost certain that the women of Mapato have it in them to overcome these challenges and strive towards their goal of financial empowerment.

The Awesome Group - A group formed after Campus.

Misnomer or not, this investment group has changed the lives of its members in its three years of steady growth. Awesome started as a group of friends from the University of Nairobi. A year out of campus in 2008, the women, as most friends do, considered contributing money to invest. This idea stewed for another two-and-a-half years. In August 2011, the eight women made "Awesome" official by starting monthly contributions of Sh2, 000. The motivation behind contributing was not to invest in land and property only but — primarily — to invest in each other. Moreover, judging from their mood and conversation during the interview, it is evident that they have achieved this goal: These newly-weds and young mothers have tagged their babies and toddlers along for their monthly meeting at a picnic site in Tigoni.

Awesome's first investment was in March 2012, and it was the purchase of a one-year government bond at Sh100, 000. The favourable market that year gave the Chama a return of Sh16, 000. While the bond matured, the Chama shifted its focus to the short-term cash needs of its members and started lending loans. The loans are at a simple interest rate of 12 per cent, with a repayment period of six months. The minimum lending amount is Sh50, 000. The cap is based on the availability of funds. To date, the group has made just under Sh150, 000 from interest on loans only.

Members share the Chama's roles: The treasurer maintains its books. A secretary documents meeting minutes. Since Awesome's constitution is not documented, these minutes are tooled for its decision-making. The investment adviser, a research analyst by profession, steers its investment decisions. What does it attribute its growing success to?

"First, it is consistency in member contributions," says Bianca Oyula, the treasurer. Individually, Sh2, 000 (now Sh3, 500) may not seem much. However, collectively, it is substantial for an investment. Also, the priority and discipline in contributions and attending meetings. Lastly, it is how the Chama has uplifted its members. Through its loan facilities, members have financed their dreams and personal projects without seeking costly bank loans. This has been the greatest measure of success for the group so far.

Being an all-women group — and friends — one cannot help asking, whether there have been any personal conflicts that have arisen.

"Yes, they have," says Wanjiku Muchiri, the chairlady. "But we have learnt to accept each other's personalities. We are friends first and we want this Chama to last a lifetime. We need each other for that." Plans?

"To register the group as a company and to grow our asset portfolio," says Joy D' Souza, the investments adviser. "Our agenda for this month's meeting is to discuss an investment in the stock market." Most importantly, to continue to invest in each other. Not only in financing our members' ambitions, but also be there to hold each other's' hands through life.

Challenge segment

➢ After reading the three Chama stories, their success and challenges, has it changed your perception about Chamas?

➢ Which of the three above do you think fits in your investment plan?

➢ Have you ever benefited from Chama's money? What problem did it help you overcome?

➢ Women seem to be doing very well in this Chama idea, how do you think men are doing?

➢ There are challenges in Chamas. Have those challenges hindered people from achieving financial independence?

Big Lessons from Illustrations above

❖ Chamas helps people achieve financial stability.

❖ Chamas have challenges but those challenges do not hinder committed people from achieving their financial goals.

❖ Unity is strength. You can achieve a lot if you join hands with others.

❖ Chamas help people to develop financial discipline.

❖ Trust, loyalty and commitment are the core values needed in any successful Chama.

❖ Chamas can shield you from unnecessary bank loans and their huge interest rates.

Chapter Ten

NEVER MIX BUSINESS WITH
FRIENDSHIP, PLEASURE & FAMILY
A good Entrepreneur is always principled. (N. Michael)

Friends are good and having fun is great but the two should never mix with business. I do not suggest that when you have a business, you should not have friends, but you should make sure that you have kept a boundary between business transactions and friendship. Your friends, including family members should understand and respect your business. For instance, money meant for business should never be used to entertain friends and relatives, unless you have planned for such entertainment. Friends taking goods on credit from your business premises without a proper agreement on how payment should be made must be discouraged. A businessperson should only use friendship as a tool of marketing and selling their products. Your friends should be your asset and not liability. A good entrepreneur is always disciplined.

By setting clear rules on how to deal with friends and relatives, you will realize that people take your business based on how you treat it. If you respect your work, everyone will also respect it. It is therefore upon you to brand your business model.

Koech's kiosk in Kangemi.

Mr Koech, (not is real name) has been running a kiosk in Kangemi since 2005. I met him first in 2007 when as a young man after high school, I was distributing cakes (Kangumu) in that area by bicycle as I waited to join college. It was a good business, which earned me my first Motorola mobile phone among other things back in the days. The good thing about Koech was that, he always kept his promise. I used to give him five packets of cakes, and we would pay me the morning of the following day. He never

63

failed. Despite his kiosk being too small, he had so many customers, to the extent that people queued for service especially in the early morning and evening hours (business rush hour). He had partitioned the kiosk into two; the front was his business section while the back was his single room.

What was Koech's Secret?

One of the factors that made Koech have many customers in his business was that he also sold milk. Someone supplied him with fresh milk from Limuru early in the morning. As the people flocked to buy fresh milk from his kiosk, they also bought bread, and cakes. With time, Koech started selling onions, kales, spinach and tomatoes. He got these not from Kangemi market but from a place called Soko Mjinga. Someone supplied them to him directly from the farm at a very cheap price which enabled him to remain competitive. When the neighbouring shops saw how successful Koech was, they upped their game by doubling their stocks and lowering prices. To make matter worse, they started selling on credit. Koech's fortunes started to fade.

Koech Greatest Lessons

Due to the neighbour's policies of lowering prices and selling on credit, Koech suffered a great setback. He could hardly make sales as before as half of his customers disappeared. Only few royal customers remained.

"It was tough time for me, I almost closed the business. My suppliers were also beginning to lose confidence in me," Koech narrated. "I was even praying, asking God to help me start another business, when some of my old customers started trickling back one by one. It had been three months of pain and frustrations, but I thank God that I was able to bounce back." When I asked him aboout the secret of winning them back; his answer was surprising.

"I did nothing. They just came back, but later on, I learned that they were running away from other shops because they had taken lot of goods on credit and most of them were not willing to pay." Koech then told me that he never gave out his goods on credit, and if he did, it was for a few

64

customers and within set limits. "I can't give someone credit of more than Ksh 500, that is the maximum limit. To some customers, the maximum limit is Ksh 200, and this is only for people I trust, but for the majority of them, I do not give credit at all. I have come to note that if you give people goods on credit, it will accumulate to the extent that they cannot pay, and that will make them run away." How will I expand my business, if people take goods on credit worth thousands?"

What about Expansion
Currently Koech has expanded his business. He has since moved to a nearby premise that has bigger space. He also owns a Toyota Probox that he uses to get milk and other farm produce in Limuru and Soko Mjinga. His wife runs the business when Koech is away. Apart from that, he is currently selling and refilling gas cylinders and also offers M-pesa services.

Our challenge Segment
➤ How do your friends treat your side hustle?
➤ Have you ever thought of setting boundaries on how friends and relatives handle your business?
➤ What has contributed to success in Koech's business?

Great lessons from Koech's story
❖ Always establish your niche.
❖ Entertaining customers with credits and very low prices is counterproductive.
❖ You can never operate a successful business if you do not balance your credit.
❖ A good business should always give the best to its customers.
❖ Always use your head to remain ahead of your competitors through innovation and creativity.
❖ Never share your business secrets to your competitors.

Chapter Eleven

LEARN, LEARN, AND
BE OPEN TO NEW IDEAS

If you refuse good advice, you are asking for trouble;
follow it and you are safe. (Proverbs 13:13)

According to Forbes, around 543,000 businesses start each month in the USA. Seven out of ten businesses survive for two years, half for five years and only a third for ten years or more. This is because they lack the right kind of knowledge needed to run a business. In Kenya, a 2016 survey by Kenya National Bureau of Statistics (KNBS) reveals that almost 400,000 micro, small and medium enterprises did not see their second anniversary for a period of five years. Most of these businesses collapse because of a decline in income, losses incurred from increased operating costs, a tough economic environment and faulty business decisions.

To run a business, it is essential to be well- prepared and loaded with the right strategies, contacts, networks and information. All these qualities can be acquired by being acquainted with the business world.

Business seminars and training help a lot in this endeavor. One of the advantages of attending a business seminar is the fact that you are likely to get advice from the experts on how to expand your business or how to re-strategize if your business is heading south. It also gives you a chance to ask difficult questions about factors that may be hindering your progress. It is fundamentally necessary to accept that most entrepreneurs' ideas never come out completely formed. A coach therefore is needed to offer the right guidance. A coach in this case is like a referee in a football match. He is able to see more than the players can see happening during the match. This makes the coach have an upper hand in guiding young entrepreneurs. If you are not willing to learn, forget about running a business.

Budding entrepreneurs should not hesitate in embracing the culture of involving experts, especially business mentors, as this will cushion them from several faulty business decisions and losses that eventually cost them their vision and investment. Though some people say that experience is the best teacher, I still hold to the one that says you can learn from other people's mistakes. No man is an island. You cannot rely on your knowledge and skills only and remain on top. It is good to be open to new ideas and to listen to how people are progressing in their business. You must learn, learn and accept being corrected by other people's mistakes.

Importance of taking part in Business seminars/ workshops/conventions/conferences, etc
Utathiaga augaga no nyina urugaga wega. (Kikuyu proverb)
He who travels not thinks only his/her mother cooks well.

It is clear from the above proverb that if you have never gone out to experience how things are done elsewhere, you live with the ignorance of being the best. This proverb brings out the idea of reading materials and articles on business, buying books on entrepreneurship, consulting your business mentors, taking time to learn from others, attending business seminars and workshops among other things.

The Benefits.
i.   Get exposed to new ideas and skills.
Running a business can become daunting if you run out of ideas. This is because good and implementable ideas do not come easily. Attending a business seminar can expand your horizon and expose you to many amazing ideas on how to carry forward with your business.

ii.   Understanding the Market.
Workshops and seminars also help you to understand the market trends. Different speakers can give you an insight into what is in high demand and where one needs to turn the business to in order to get better returns. Sometimes, the speakers highlight the changing trends in the markets, the latest technology among other things. The conference can also give you a

chance to meet your competitors and learn about their strategies. This will help you re-organise your business in order to deal with competition.

iii. Help You to Discover your Strengths and Weaknesses.

One can never know their strengths and weaknesses until they figure out how other successful businesses in the same field are performing. You may be selling two thousands litres of milk per month as a farmer only to discover that, there are other farmers who are selling a million litres of the same plus other products. When you notice the difference, you are able to identify the weaknesses in your strategies. You are also able to know and build on what you have been doing right.

iv. Network Building.

One of the most crucial traits of any successful business is its wide network of clients and vendors. Business seminars can be a blessing because it brings business people under one roof. It gives an opportunity to meet with potential vendors and exchange talks with them. With a good strategy and effective communication skills, it is possible to convince them to work with you. You can also get a chance to meet with new customers.

v. Immense Knowledge.

Business seminars are usually organised by professionals. Only business experts get a chance to address the gathering, thus you are going to get a lot of new facts and skills on how to run and improve your business from these experts. Knowledge pertaining to reducing the cost of running the business, better management skills, hiring the right employees and how to find new clients rarely miss on the training package.

vi. Pick Crucial Inspirations.

Speakers usually inspire people with practical examples, facts and other things. You are likely to get your inspiration from such talk and get re-energised. This will fuel you to face your business with renewed zest and enthusiasm necessary to motivate your progress towards success.

vii. It gives you a sense of Belonging.

Running a small business can be quite lonely, and it can often feel as though you are struggling in isolation. Events such as small business conferences, conventions, seminars and workshops offer opportunities to escape the bubble and connect with like-minded business people, many of whom are dealing with the exact challenges and eager to share their experiences. Discussing your challenges with others in a similar position creates a chance for collective problem solving, and you will almost certainly feel less alone in your endeavour.

viii.   Opportunity to Boost Reputation.
If you happen to give a presentation at such events as a guest speaker, it can establish you as a thoughtful leader in your niche. This will position you as an expert, increase your personal profile, raise awareness of your brand and boost your reputation within your industry. It also helps to build your confidence in your endeavors.

Note.
Investing the time and money to attend to a conference, convention, seminar, or trade show relevant to your business will almost guarantee that you return home with new tools, fresh ideas, inspiration, valuable contacts and a renewed approach that will help you to become a more effective and efficient entrepreneur. If you are not able to attend such events, grab a book, movie, or watch live business shows. Business magazines and articles can also expand your ideas in business matters. The bottom line is that you must learn if you want success in business.

The challenge segment.
➢ No man is an island. How does this impact on how you handle new ideas and challenges.
➢ How beneficial will it be for you, if you take part in a business conference?
➢ If you are not in the position of attending to seminars, workshops, conventions and the like, what other options do you have?
➢ What is the importance of consulting a coach, mentor or a business expert?

The Big Lessons

- ❖ A good entrepreneur is the one willing to learn and is open to new ideas, challenges, and technologies.
- ❖ Business workshops and seminars can open more opportunities for business.
- ❖ Attending business events equips you with new skills and ideas crucial in improving your business.
- ❖ Rejecting new ideas is likely to make your business stagnate.
- ❖ Consulting experts, coaches, and mentors is crucial for any successful entrepreneur.

Chapter Twelve

THE MONITORING EYE:
TAKE CHARGE OF YOUR BUSINESS
Unmonitored Business is a Lost Venture. (N.Michael)

One of the greatest mistakes that young and inexperienced entrepreneurs make is leaving their investments unmonitored or delegating this responsibility to other people. Some people, out of laziness and greed for quick cash open up business ventures and abandon them to be managed by other people. The results are always predictable: the business collapses within no time. If you have no time to follow on your investment, you will soon discover that it is no more. Most small-scale businesses like shops, kiosks et al require personal touch. Employing someone to manage such small-scale business may not do. This does not mean that you cannot start a business if you are working, but you have to first establish the checks and balances of how monitoring is going to be done. If you do not put up these measures, you will discover that you have nothing to manage.

The nature of business, dictates the mode of supervision. Some demand daily supervision, others weekly, but the shorter the period the better. It is also important to note that employees may not share in your vision for the business. This means that they may not have enthusiasm to run the business as the owner would want it run. Some of them, in fact majority of them are there because of the salary. It is therefore important to take your time to study carefully the people you have employed there and select the honest and committed ones as supervisors of others. Let the supervisor do their work as you closely monitor all of them. Never put the supervisors in charge of everything. It is your responsibility to make the venture successful.

As you study your employees, they are also studying you and sooner or later, they will discover your weaknesses and exploit them. Therefore as a boss, you are supposed to remain alert all the time. Remember that some of your employees may be using your business premises to do their personal businesses.

Benefits of Regular Business Monitoring
The cost of preventing mistakes is generally much less than the cost of correcting mistakes. (Business Quote.)

i.   Helps to provide Management insights.

Business reports collate much data around your business venture. This data provides crucial information for business management. Insights around spending, growth and profits are useful in creating future projections, marketing plans and budgets. Business reports also provide crucial leads for tracking business growth. Employees should always prepare regular reports especially on sales for close monitoring of the business. If this does not happen, your business will fall.

ii.   Identifying Problems.

Routine monitoring and reporting are important as they aid in the process of identifying gaps in a business venture. When such gaps are noted, the owners or the management are able to address them before they escalate to big issues. Monitoring an area that has problems and comparing data collected over time should help point out what has triggered the issue. This is then used to provide a way to fix the problem.

iii.   Highlighting Opportunities.

Reports in a business help in tracking the past successes. These achievements can be used to define future growth opportunities. The company or an individual is able to identify what worked well and what more could be done in the future.

iv.   Transparency.

For a big company, annual reporting is a legality. For smaller firms and personal businesses, regular reporting can offer additional transparency throughout the year. This will set the pace for growth. It also makes the business appear more attractive to potential investors.

v. Setting Goals.

Reporting on business performance ensures that performance over different periods are compared. Whatever the results, identifying trends in the business over time helps in setting future goals.

The story of Miss Makau and her Pharmacy Business

Miss Makau (not her real name) graduated from college in November 2017 with a diploma in pharmacy. Luckily, she had saved some Ksh 40,000 by the time she was graduating. This together with the money she garnered during her graduation amounted to Ksh 50,000. It was like winning a rotary. She had always dreamed of owning her own pharmacy. Therefore, in January 2018 she left home in Mumbuini to Machakos town in search of business premises. Before long, she came across a big pharmacy in one of the streets in Machakos run by a young man, Mutua. She approached him to enquire where she could get a vacant shop.

Miss Makau gets Lucky.

"What are you planning to start, a boutique or what? Matua asked. Miss Makau informed her that she was interested in opening a pharmacy. As they were conversing, a plump woman who probably was listening to their conversation from a room inside the pharmacy emerged. Her husband was the owner of the pharmacy and Mutua was their employee. The couple was planning to relocate to Nairobi since the husband, who is a doctor had gotten a job at Kenyatta National Hospital. The pharmacy was therefore on sale. Miss Makau told them she was interested in buying the pharmacy and that she would be back soon after consulting with her father who is a primary school teacher in Machakos Primary.

That Saturday afternoon, the four sat in one of the restaurants in Machakos to discuss the business. The stock in the business was worth Ksh 150,000 plus goodwill of Ksh 30,000. In total, the doctor and her wife were asking for Ksh180, 000 in cash. Miss Makau and her father had only Ksh 50,000. The negotiations were tough, but finally the doctor and his wife agreed on Ksh 20,000 for goodwill, bringing it down to Ksh 170,000, to be be paid in three instalment. The first instalment was agreed to be Ksh 70,000 and the rest to be paid in two instalment for a period of six months. That translated to Ksh 50,000 in three months' time. They signed the papers and the deal was done. Miss Makau father had to add Ksh 20,000 to support her daughter in making the first payment.

Mutua becomes Jobless.

Mutua now had no job. Miss Makau could not afford to employ someone considering her commitment to repaying the debt. The business did well, and within the first six months, she was able to foot the balance. The big problem was that after paying the debt, she was not able to purchase most of the drugs, and now the pharmacy was headed to a collapse. Miss Makau was in desperate need of cash. As she was about to close it down, she received a call from Machakos County Government to attend an interview for a job she had applied a year earlier. Luckily, she passed her interview and was posted to Machakos Hospital. She took a loan of Ksh 200,000 and restocked the Pharmacy. She was sure that within a year, she would have her money back, considering her experience in the area.

Mutua is hired again.

Mutua was called back to run the business. Things went smoothly for the first month, but from the second month, business was very bad. Miss Makau could not meet her business targets. When she took the stock, she realized that drugs were not moving. What happened to her customers? She started fearing that Mutua could either be overcharging the or mishandling them. She decided to investigate.

The Decisive Moment.

One day, Miss Makau took a day off from work and arrived at her pharmacy around 11:00a.m. To her surprise, Mutua was not in the pharmacy, but another woman was standing behind the counter-serving customers. Miss Makau thought she was dreaming. She was fuming with anger and was about to scream, but due to her business etiquette, she held herself. After all, the customers had done nothing wrong. The woman informed her what she knew - the pharmacy belonged to Mutua. It was not the first time for her to work in that pharmacy. Mutua usually gave her the job when he was going to get drugs or new supplies. He used to sell his own drugs using her premises, but still being paid every month. As they were talking, he emerged carrying three cartons. Miss Makau had to fire him. It was very painful. She spent the next four days installing CCTV Cameras and other security equipment and control measures in the pharmacy. She also hired someone else to run the business, under new guidelines and serious surveillance. She had learned her lesson.

Challenge Segment
➤ What would you say are the advantages of monitoring your investment?
➤ What is the greatest challenge of Miss Makau's investment?
➤ What do you think is the role of CCTV cameras in business monitoring?
➤ Employees cannot always be trusted to run your business, why is this?
➤ If you have to succeed in business, you have to know where your money is all time. Do you believe in this assertion?
➤ According to your understanding of business matters, how would you ensure checks and balances in your business?

The Big Lessons
❖ If you need to succeed in business, monitoring is necessary.
❖ Do not put full trust in your employee to run your business.
❖ Regular reports from the employees are crucial is setting the future goal of your business venture.
❖ CCTV Cameras are essential in business monitoring.
❖ It is your personal responsibility to push the development agenda of your business.
❖ Some employees do not share the same vision with their employer. They are just there for a salary.

Chapter Thirteen

YOU CAN MAKE IT
IN FARMING
There is one thing stronger than all the armies of the world:
and that is an idea whose time has come. (Victor Hugo)

The problem among Kenyan youths is lack knowledge in agriculture or farming. In high school, for example you will find that most bright students do not take agriculture. Most of them think that since they are good in academics, they do not see themselves being farmers in the future. This negative attitude towards agriculture has led to thousands of young university and college graduates flocking in the cities looking for white-collar jobs, leaving behind acres of unutilised land in their rural areas. What a shock? It is not unusual to find a young man from Kakamega, Kiambu, Muranga or any other agriculturally rich regions in Kenya struggling in Nairobi while at home, the family has acres of unused land. The most traumatic cases is where students who took agriculture related courses go to the city to look for employment. African students still cling to the 17th century idea that farming is tedious and dirty because most of them are not acquainted with *smart farm* which has made agriculture more efficient, enjoyable and easy.

What is a Smart Farm?

Smart farming and precision agriculture involve the integration of advanced technologies into the existing farming practices in order to increase production efficiency and quality. As an added benefit, they also improve the quality of life for farm workers by reducing heavy labour and tedious tasks. Among the technologies available for the present day farmers, include:

✓ Sensing technologies, including soil scanning, water, light, humid

and temperature management.
- ✓ Software applications - specialised software solutions that target specific farm types.
- ✓ Communication technologies, such as cellular communications.
- ✓ Positioning technologies, including GPS.
- ✓ Hardware and software systems that enable Internet of Things(IoT) based solutions, robotics and automation.
- ✓ Data analysis, that underlies the decision-making and predication processes.

Smart farm idea is not new in Kenya and Africa in general. If a person is interested, he/she can get more information about it online. There are also smart farm magazines, applications, Television programmes, et al.

Agribusiness in Kenya

What is Agribusiness?
Agribusiness is the business of agricultural production. Majority of existing agribusinesses in Kenya can be started without any professional training. To run a successful agricultural business, you need to familiarize yourself with the opportunities available, the threats you can face and the returns of your venture. You can also visit your county agricultural offices to inquire about funding. If you feel that you need some special training in any farming method, log in to [eLengo Online Farm Course]. There are also several applications that you can download to guide you on market trends in Kenyan.

The size of land is not a big issue
Eight Profitable farming ventures on just ¼ acre of land in Kenya.
Advice on Farming by Mr Paul Mbugua Njuguna on Kuza Hub July 2016.
When it comes to farming in Kenya and Africa, land is one of our biggest problems unlike in the West. Some farmers have no clear land ownership rights. This means that they cannot pledge the property as collateral

for financing to scale their farms. Young professionals and the youth are starting to see agribusiness as a viable venture. This is a good thing, but for those looking to farm, land is one of the first things you have to figure out especially for the urbanites. So, what farming ventures can be done profitably on a ¼ acre of land? Here are eight different types of farming you can consider.

1) Mushroom farming

Mushroom farming is not very old in Kenya. Cultivation used to be a complex affair but things have been made much simpler for farmers through numerous research, training, and workshops. There have also been workarounds in the process and introduction of more tolerant varieties like Oyster. They do not require a huge piece of land compared to other crops. A quarter acre of land is enough to have an incubation house and a cropping house. You can make use of the vertical space too since mushrooms do not grow tall. If you have 1000 bags in one cropping room, you can get close to 2 tons of button mushrooms going at an average of Ksh600/kg. This translates to about Ksh1.2 Million.

Mushrooms are sold to supermarkets, hotels and households. Recently, there has been demand for mushrooms from Uganda. The demand is big at 1200 tons a year according to NAFIS where only half of it is met. Dominance is by large-scale producers mainly exporting. With proper marketing, this is one profitable venture and you will require less capital in comparison to others.

2) Garlic farming

Garlic is a high value horticultural crop. It is part of the onion family. Garlic is loved for its flavor in food and health benefits. It does well in optimum conditions and under good care. Garlic takes about 6 months to harvest. A ¼ acre of land can give you about 2.5 tons yield of garlic bulb selling at a farm gate price of around Ksh150/kg. There is demand from both local and export market. Garlic requires adequate skills, training and good research to do well. You will need to understand the local varieties, get certified seeds, good soil and best environment. Growing organic garlic is preferred especially for the export market.

3) Fish farming

Kenya used to depend on lakes and rivers for fish in the past, but not anymore. Commercial fish farming has taken off where fish are reared in ponds. The African catfish, Nile tilapia and the rainbow trout are the popular breeds. It is not hard to start a fish farm, you just need training. You can have 100-meter square ponds fit in a quarter of an acre for breeding. The main costs in fish farming are labour, polythene, feeds and the fingerlings. The ponds can also be made of Fibre, concrete and plastic but these will cost more. You also need to consider the climate, suitable land, fish species, pond design, feeds and the market.

The demand for fish has been going up with more people consuming white meat locally. Fish sells for about Ksh500/kg and for ¼ an acre you can have a few thousands of them. The catfish is fast growing and can weigh over 15kgs. Tilapia can be harvested when they weigh 250g. By use of modern fish farming techniques, production can be maximized.

Note: You need a proper research on the market since currently, there are fish being exported from China. We hope this import will come to end soon, so that our local market can improve. However, the demand is huge, and there is still a chance of getting your market locally.

4) Poultry farming

Poultry involves rearing chicken, which can be indigenous (Kienyeji), layers, or broilers. Improved indigenous breeds are also available to farmers. Other birds can also be reared like quail and guinea fowl but chicken is more popular in Kenya taking 98%. Chicken eggs are consumed more than meat in Kenya. Chicken meat has hotels as their biggest market.

The appropriate structure can fit in a ¼ acre and make a profitable business. Make sure the housing is up to recommended standards. There is a need to focus on marketing your produce by targeting large hotels, supermarkets, schools, export, etc. The indigenous (Kienyeji) chicken can be sold for around Ksh1000 in the market. When doing poultry farming, attention to details and proper knowledge is necessary for a successful venture.

Note: Be careful about quail farming since its market is not predictable.

5) Passion fruit farming

Passion fruit is one of the biggest fruit exports in Kenya. The local market demand is also quite high. They can be consumed fresh or the pulp used for making juice and other products e.g. yoghurt. There are two popular types in Kenya: the purple variety that grows in high altitudes and the yellow variety that has higher yields and is disease resistant.

A ¼ acre can grow about 350 passion plants or more. One plant with good care can produce 10–15 kg of fruits in a year. Passion fruits sell for Ksh 40–100/kg while Grade 1 for export can go for around Ksh70–100/kg. Passion fruit farming has become popular in Kenya. For example the North Rift farmers are moving away from maize to passion fruits which has better returns, cheaper to maintain and have a ready market going as far as Uganda. The passion plant is a climber, which means there can be creative ways of maximizing on the little space you have.

6) Greenhouse farming

A greenhouse is what some people would call an almost perfect farm. This is because it provides a controlled environment that best suits the growth of crops. They are an enclosure in which moisture content and temperatures can be regulated. Your crops are also protected from the outside menace of insects, rodents and other animals. This means greenhouse farmers can farm all year round, in and out of season. The most popular greenhouse crops are; courgettes, tomatoes, capsicums, cucumbers, cabbages, and other vegetables, which are high value crops. Yields in a greenhouse are higher compared to open field farming for the same space utilized.

Green houses come in different sizes as small as 20M by 6M, which you can fit, easily on your ¼-acre piece of land. This will cost you between Ksh100, 000 to Ksh150, 000. The starting capital may look much but considering you will be farming all year round with reduced risks, it is totally worth it. Before you rush in, plan and consider the full cost of setup, crops you will grow and after- sales support from the greenhouse vendor.

7) Dairy farming

Dairy farming can be very profitable but there is a certain fear when it comes to keeping dairy cows. There are successful farmers making millions out of dairy farming. It can be practiced in both high and low lands. Varieties of dairy cattle common in Kenya are Jersey, Friesian, Ayrshire, Guernsey and cross breeds. What you need is patience with your cows, a good setup, good feeds, proper cow management and technical support from a good vet and nutritionist.

The feeds alone account for about 40–60% total cost. With ¼ an acre, you can keep more than three dairy cows. Three cows producing an average of 30 litres of milk a day can give you Ksh1 million in a year if you sell milk at a price of Ksh 30. Good breeds will give a farmer 30–50 litres of milk a day. Be very attentive to details when it comes to dairy farming and get good support. Co-operatives buy milk at relatively lower prices, but their market is guaranteed. Alernatively, you can sell your milk to other institutions at a better price or sell directly from the farm to vendors.

8) Bee keeping

According to National Farmers Information Service(NAFIS), only 20% of the potential 100,000 metric tons per year of honey production has been tapped. Demand for honey and other bee products is high. 80% of Kenya's land is arid and semi-arid and has abundant flora, which makes it perfect for bee keeping.

Bee keeping requires a small space compared to other crops. You can have 50 colonies of bees in only ¼ acre of land and the best thing is it does not need to be fertile or need rain. There are good beehives that can give you about 9–13 kg of honey per harvest and can be harvested 6–10 times a year. Keeping bees is actually cheaper in terms of labor and is less competitive bearing in mind that it does not compete for the same resources with other types of farming.

A quarter acre of land can do much when it comes to farming, so do not limit yourself and start small. You can start learning how to cultivate mushrooms on Kuza.

The story of Boniface Bundi (Kenyan)
Agriculture is the most healthful, most useful and most noble employment of man. (George Washington)

Boniface Bundi earned his first million from the soil. The University of Nairobi graduate says he put his marketing degree papers aside, picked up a shovel and started digging for money, metaphorically. He decided to pursue farming and he has never looked back.

"I started by growing French beans (Michiri). I had my fingers crossed that all would go well," he says. That was in 2011, right after he had graduated from the university. He asked his parents for a parcel of land to try his hand in farming. He was broke, and his only hope was his passion in farming and the marketing skills he had gained from his course in the University. His love for farming was cultivated by his father, Stephen M'kuura who he describes as a role model and pacesetter. He grew up watching his father, a Class 7 dropout farm the land and use the proceeds to educate him and his two siblings. Though his father missed the opportunity to further his education, he endeavored to see all his children attain higher education. As a teenager, the love for farming had been inculcated in him. He was sure he would become a farmer, no matter the direction his education took him. "Even though I got a marketing job in the motor industry, I would still go home after work and take care of my crops, " he says.

Five years down the line, Bundi says that he earns an average of KSh. 200,000 per month from his farm. He has expanded his michiri farm and now grows it for export. On average, he harvests 800 Kgs of michiri a week, and sells it to an export company. He also has two dairy cows from which he gets about 40 litres of milk daily. He sells the milk to hotels in Meru. His recent addition to the farm include potatoes and tomatoes.

Challenges and Setbacks.

His desire to step up and do more than his father ever did in his heyday when he managed the farm has also had some setbacks. His fortunes have been interrupted by the drought and he had had to outsource water from boreholes in the neighborhood. "The drought reality hit me when I saw my crops starting to wilt. I knew I had to act fast or lose everything," he says. The prolonged dry season caused a streak of hopelessness on him and the farmers around him, as they were not sure if their farms would flourish.

"Cows need a lot of food and the price of feeds has gone up, so we have to dig deep into our pockets to keep them alive. It is worrying, because we don't know how long it will last," he says. The drought has also brought with it crop pests, especially on his French beans (michiri) which are a challenge to contain.

Bundi was enthusiastic when he set up a greenhouse last year. He thought it would yield great profits, catapult him to the Millionaires' Club, and probably earn him fame as one of the most successful farmers in Meru. Sadly, his dreams were crashed. Within a few weeks, the crops he had planted wilted and died. He was left wallowing in losses he had not foreseen, and was almost thrown into a mire of hopelessness. He attributes the losses to not conducting research before embarking on the greenhouse project.

"I did not have enough knowledge of what is needed to run a greenhouse. I thought I needed the same skills I had used in my farm," he says. He has not given up on the project. He wants to start afresh. He has been consulting experts who know what it takes to be a successful greenhouse farmer.

"**Farming is learning.** You can never know it all, so you have to be ready to ask," he says. His eyes light up when he talks about his other passion – music. Besides farming, he also dedicates his time composing songs and performing in functions at a fee. He is a gospel musician who draws inspiration from his father who was a church instrumentalist. His childhood was defined by the sound of his father strumming a guitar, and humming along gospel songs while encouraging them to join in.

"I would watch him passionately playing his instruments and creating good music. I knew I have to be a musician," Bundi says. Every beat he plays, every song he sings, is an ode to his father who taught him to crash through barriers and follow through everything his mind conceives.

"My father may not have had a good education, but he did his best to encourage us to follow our dreams," he says.

It has been five years sweating in the farm, falling and rising again. He has made profits, much more than he anticipated when he started. **He still believes farming is the best employer**. He has now collaborated with his friend, and they have bought land. The duo hopes to take farming to a higher level by growing more crops for export.

Bundi's Advise to Young People.

To his fellow youth still waiting for white-collar jobs he says: **"If only young people knew how much they can get from farming. They would not spend most of their days worrying about where to get jobs."**

The challenge segment

➢ Do you agree with Boniface that farming is the best employer?
➢ From the story of Boniface Bundi, how can you as a farmer avoid getting losses in your farming business?
➢ Farming is learning. How truthful is this assertion to you as a college or university graduate?
➢ If you are to start agribusiness today, which one suits you?
➢ What do you think about Smart Farm mode of farming?
➢ Most graduates are languishing in poverty in the cities, while unutilized land is being wasted in the rural areas. What is your take on this?
➢ Do you personally think you can make it in farming?
➢ Thorough research is needed when planning to invest in greenhouses farming. What are your personal experiences with greenhouse farmers?

The Big Lessons

❖ Smart farmand agribusiness is the way to go for young school leavers.
❖ You can make good money from farming.
❖ You do not need a lot of land to engage in farming.
❖ People from arid and semi-arid areas can make money through bee keeping.

- ❖ Farming has its own challenges but through learning, there is a great chance of success.
- ❖ There are many options to choose from if you are ready to try your hand in farming?
- ❖ If you need to be educated, you can take courses on eLengo online Farm Courses and other online platforms.
- ❖ If you do not have enough land to do farming, you can always lease one.

Chapter Fourteen

THE LOAN MENTALITY

If you know the value of money, go and try to borrow some: for he that goes a borrowing goes a sorrowing. (Benjamin Franklin.)

It is sad to note that we are in a world where people are living in unnecessary debts, majorly occasioned by people wanting to live beyond their means. This is extremely dangerous because a loan possesses the power to change your life for good or make you a slave for life. At a personal level, I will not advise people to take loans from financial institutions unless they intend to do some wortwhile investments from it. It does not matter whether it is a mobile money transfer loan or a huge loan from a bank or Sacco. Always avoid loans unless you need money urgently for an emergency. Remember that whatever the case, a loan not invested to generate income will always leave you poorer. This means that the more loans you take for other purposes other than for business purposes, the poorer you become.

Banks and start-ups.

Banks rarely give loans to starters since they understand the risks involved in start-ups. They usually need security e.g. salary, provision of collateral et al. The interest rates are usually high and most of the starters may not have the financial muscles to cope with them. I advice small-scale business starters to avoid starting with a loan at all costs. Let the loan come when you have learned some tricks about your business and when you have started to make some profits. Starting up a business using a loan is very risky especially for someone who does not have another source of income. If anything happens, the bank will come for you. So start small, gain some business skills and attract more customers, and consider a small loan to expand your venture after that . Business is about moving gradually, as you learn the market trends. So always bite what you can chew. Taking huge loans can choke your business to death. The bottom line is that loans should be used towards investment.

The power of a Business Location
"The three most important things in retail are location, location and location." (Jeff Bezos)

Five key factors when choosing a location.

The success of small scale-businesses is mostly dependent on its location. You must have it right as a small scale retailer. Although the location will be dependent on the type of business, getting it wrong on location is losing on business. There are various factors to consider when choosing a business location. These include:

i. Accessibility. Does your business rely on frequent deliveries? If so, it is important to consider the local transport links, particularity main roads and motorways. This will ensure that your daily business operations are not hampered by poor transport links. Another factor on accessibility is whether your customers can easily get into your premises. A business is better if it is located where there is flow of people. Take for instance a restaurant that is located on the front side of a Central Business District (CBD) and another one located behind the shops. Which one is accessible to more people? Of course the one on the front side. The shops located on the front side of building may be charged expensively when it comes to rent but they also make more money as compared to those located in the backstreet. If your business relies on high customer footfall, then ensuring your business is accessible by cars and buses will be an important consideration. For most retail businesses, your foot traffic is extremely important. You do not want to be tucked away in a corner where shoppers are likely to bypass you. On the other hand, if your business requires confidentiality, you may not want it located in a high profile traffic area.

ii. Security. - Believe it or not, your location can increase your odds of being affected by crime, which can influence your insurance premiums, as well as the additional measures you may need to take to secure your business premises. Since you are there to make profit and not to invest in sophisticated security measures, always locate your business in an area with low crime rates. For example in Kenya, an M-pesa shop located in some streets in Kayole, an area with a higher crime rate has a higher chance of being robbed as compared to the same business located in Westlands, Nairobi. Your business premises must also be well constructed with secure doors and windows. Permanent structures (stone buildings) are safer compared to iron-sheet structures.

iii. Competition. If you locate your business in an area where there is so much competition from established businesses, you risk failing in getting customers. Unless you have something special to offer, avoid such locations. On the other hand, your proximity to other competing business could be crucial to your success. You are likely to discover their weaknesses and capitalise on them to gain customers. There are exceptions in this rule. Some businesses like car dealers prefer being near each other so that the customers can compare the best available cars. If you have a unique product from a new innovation, choosing an area that already has a ripe market could work to your advantage. However, if you realize that your competitor is going to make your job tougher, look elsewhere.

iv. Cost of Doing Business. It is very important to survey on average costs of business, ranging from business licences and premises. Hidden charges like deposits, parking fees etc, need to be given serious considerations. ~~Estimating the living cost of the location will prevent a commitment outside your means.~~ If by any means you cannot afford a premise, consider establishing your small business in an open market. If it is an office, locate it in a place whose rent you can comfortably pay without a strain.

v. Potential for growth/expansion. You need to determine whether your business premises can accommodate business growth or a spike of demands. Moving from one premise to another is an expensive affair that could even make you lose customers. A decision must therefore be made on whether the premise you are choosing is a short-term location or if you will stay there for the long haul.

Thomas Shop Business in Kangemi

Kangemi is one of the most densely populated places in Kenya, which is both the bane of, and to some extent a boon to the residents. Back in 2007, I was in this town selling cakes (Kangumu) when I met Thomas Mwaniki. He had completed high school in 2004 and had been lucky to get a job in one of the biggest supermarkets in Nairobi.

Just like any other young man who looks forward to progress in life, he had embarked on a chronic saving mechanism. Out of his salary of fifteen thousand, he saved ten because he used to live with one of his relatives who was also a senior manager in the supermarket. By December 2006, Thomas had saved around Ksh 360,000. He called his host relative and told him that he was resigning to start his own venture.

Thomas landed in Kangemi with the big idea of starting a mini-supermarket. Kangemi was his dream town due to its huge population. He intended to apply the policy of one-step at a time to grow his small business into an empire. He had gathered all the necessary information regarding running a supermarket: the supply chain, arrangement of items et al. The only thing that he had not figured out was the business premises. He had friends in Kangemi, so getting a business premises in the area was not a big deal.

Thomas is Shocked.

With one of his friends, Thomas started looking for a good site. That was in January 2007. Most of the shops on the busy main streets were occupied, and the vacant ones were very expensive. According to the kind of premise he wanted, most of them were asking between Ksh 15,000 -18,000. This is not what the young man had anticipated.

Thomas Decides to Settle For Less

To make the story short, he decided to settle on an old house near Kangemi slum. It was big enough to host his mini-supermarket and the rent was manageable at Ksh. 8000 per month. The only problem of this house was that it was not located on the main road where majority of the people were passing. Thomas stocked the mini-supermarket and waited for customers. Business was slow. Thomas could count the number of customers who visited his new supermarket. For the first few months, he could only afford to pay rent and remain with very little.

Thomas between the Rock and a hard place Situation.

Nearing the end of 2007, things turned from bad to worse. Most of his customers came from the slums, and towards the election period, they travelled upcountry. Thomas could hardly pay the rent. Many perishables were going bad, causing huge loses by the day. One month to the general election, Thomas closed his business, sold all the remaining stock and went back home in Nyeri. He had incurred a loss of over Ksh 150,000. In 2010 when I visited the location, his old shop had been demolished and a new building was going up.

When I called him, Thomas informed me that the location did not favour his business. "I left Kangemi in 2007. I had a lot of hope in the town, but the location of my business was not strategic."

"What are you doing now in Nyeri?" I asked him.

"Currently I am operating a wholesale shop and things are okay, but my dream of owning a huge supermarket one day is still there. In fact as we speak, am working on something." He concluded. He learnt his lesson about business location, something that I believe has shaped his current business.

The challenge Segment
➢ Bank loans are important but very risky to starters. Why?
➢ Getting it wrong in business location is losing business. Why?
➢ Why do we have to consider security when choosing a business location?
➢ What is wrong with Thomas business plan?
➢ How do elections politics in Kenya impact on business?

The Great Lessons

❖ It is safer to start a business on your savings as compared to loans. Look at the case of Thomas.
❖ Banks are very hesitant in lending money to starters.
❖ A good business plan must consider location of a business.
❖ Elections politics in Kenya influences most businesses negatively.
❖ Security of business is very important consideration when one is selecting a business site.

Chapter Fifteen

YOU CAN MAKE IT
EVEN WHEN EMPLOYED

Your attitude determines your altitude

The major problem with employed people is negative attitude towards entrepreneurship. For quite sometime now, I have been thinking and asking myself, Why are some people more successful in business than others? This is a mind-intriguing question that we all have pondered at a certain time in life. I am of the opinion that it all lies in our attitude.

According to Denis Waitler, an American writer and a motivational speaker , **"Your attitude is either the lock on or key to the door of your success."** Personally, I come from the school of thought that success starts in the mind of an individual. What I mean is that if you have a clear vision or a dream about what you want to achieve in life, you can somehow visualize how you will accomplish the dream. On the other hand, if you do not have a vision, you lack the motivation and direction to accomplish anything.

Helen Keller once said that, **"The only thing worse than being blind is having sight but no vision."** Sadly, this is the case with majority of people in employment. Some, sorry to say, are so satisfied with their payslips to the extent that they compare to fattened pigs waiting for slaughter. Many of them have a negative attitude towards starting a business, mainly because they feel that they do not have time and energy to manage a business venture as most of their time and energy are spent in their jobs. Research has shown that it is very difficult to attain financial independence without a form of investment. Investment is the only antidote to financial deficiency. That being the case, even people in employment should think about investment.

How to get involved if employed
Eight Pillars of Getting Involved for Those in Employment.
  a) **Start saving.**
  Do not save what is left after spending, but spend what is left after saving. (Warren Buffett)

It does not matter how much money you earn. If you have to start a business, you must be willing to set some money aside for investment. One mistake that you should never make is saving blindly. Do not save for the sake of saving. For a good saving model, you must always have a target and a reason behind it, otherwise you are likely to misuse your savings for things not intended. If you realize that you have problem in making commitment to your saving, then you can employ the following methods.

  i) **Direct deductions by the bank/Sacco.** Deduct a portion of your salary directly from your payslip through your bank or Sacco for a period.

  ii) **Take a loan and acquire property.** Take a loan and acquire property that generates income or a property that appreciates in value, such that you can sell it later at a profit. A good example is land, buildings et al

  iii) **Join a saving groups such as Chamas.** Self-help groups like chamas can help you accumulate money for capital or acquire properties.

  iv) **Save with reputable insurance.** You can save for 2-3 years with insurance companies.

Note.

Be careful about insurance companies. Never take a premium for more than five years unless you want to spend your whole life fattening insurance companies with your payslip. If possible, avoid them completely. It is also good to do your calculations to determine the pros and cons of insurance premiums. There are myriad options for saving, so be wise on this. According to my experience with insurance companies, the only safer option is the money market.

How to enhance your saving.
For you to be in a position to save money, you must adjust accordingly

so that your life can continue smoothly.

a) **Reduce rent expenses.** Make sure you do not use all your money on rent. If possible consider living with your parents, roommate, etc. You can also consider living in a lower rent area where houses are cheaper. The rule is to spend a fixed amount of your income on housing. The general recommendation is 30% of your gross monthly income (before tax) on rent. This means that of your gross pay is Ksh 40,000, your rent should be about Ksh, 12,000. If your gross is 30,000, your rent should not exceed Ksh 9000. If possible, let the rent be even 20% of your gross salary.

Living in an expensive house does not add value to your life. If fact it is likely to drag you into the path of poverty while the property owner is smiling all the way to the bank.

b) **Do not live beyond your means**. Avoid accumulating things that add no value to your financial independence. Things like cars, expensive furniture and expensive vocations et al. These things can wait. Unless your job really demands them, avoid them completely. If you have to plan for an outing, save money for it or go to places that are within your means. If you have to buy a car, drive a car of your league: the one you can fuel and repair comfortably.

c) **Avoid Debts.** As said earlier, any money you borrow at an interest for any other purpose other than investment leaves you poorer. So avoid loans, including unnecessary mobile phone loans.

d) **Make your savings multiply.** You can do this my either investing in the money market, or in a fixed account that earns you some interests.

e) **Manage your shopping.** If you have to make it in saving, you must control how you shop and where you go for shopping. First, only buy those things that are essential for your health and well-being. Avoid accumulating so many unnecessary things in your house. Another thing to look at is the place you do your shopping. Avoid those high ends shops where goods are a bit expensive than in the ordinary market. This will help you sail through when you are saving.

f) Control your Entertainment. Cut your spending on entertainment. Avoid beer parties and drinking sprees, as this will not spare your wallet. If you cannot afford DSTV, channels, switch to free to air or cheaper ones like Startimes. If you have to go out with friends, it should not be daily. Use your car when attending to important functions to save on fuel consumption. If you can help it, use public transport sometimes.

b) Just Start.
"Only put off until tomorrow what you are willing to die having left undone." (Wise Saying)
Procrastination is the killer of dreams. Avoid postponing your investment plans. All you need is to have a simple business plan. As said earlier, it is always good to get into a business that you understand and that you have a passion for. Believe in yourself, and if possible, use the skills that you have acquired in your workplace to manage and better your business. Do not wait until you are forty to start investing; the earlier the better. "You never know what results will come from your action. But if you do nothing, there will be no results." (Mahatma Gandhi)

c) Do not be afraid of Mistakes.
Cowards die many times before their deaths; the valiant never taste of death but once. (Wise Saying)
You will never succeed in any business venture if you are always afraid of making mistakes. Mistakes are there to be made. In addition, they are part of your learning and growth. There is also nothing like understanding it all in business. No one is perfect when it comes to money, and sometimes making money mistakes allows us to learn and progress. The same applies in our daily lives. You are not going to have a perfect day every time; failures can sometimes lead to life's greatest successes.

d) Combine Faith with Actions.
Faith without action is dead. (Bible Quote)

You cannot just sit there and expect things to work out. Kikuyus have this saying that, "Ciakorire Wacu mugunda." *(It found Wacu in the farm).* This proverb originates from a story of Wacu, the most despised amongst the wives of a rich man who never gave her any presents. One day, when a banquet was being held at home, Wacu went to work in the field, since she knew that there would be nothing for her at home. In the middle of the banquet, a raven swooped down in the courtyard where the meat was being roasted and snatched a big piece and brought it to Wacu. Wacu ate to her full and took the remaining to her kids. She received her share as she worked in the field. The same principle applies to business. Your financial breakthrough cannot find you in a staffroom, office or at home doing nothing. If you are engaged in nothing, it will find those who are busy putting their faith into actions.

e) Put God First.
You cannot believe in your dreams if you do not believe in the giver of the dream. In all things, put God first. He is willing to put you ahead for excellence. (Ayivor)

You cannot ignore the power of God in your financial equations. The power of prayers for doors to open is very important. However, you should understand that God does not condone laziness and ignorance. God blesses the work of our hands. That should be in your prayer. The problem, when it comes to business and religion is that most people try to bribe God with their offerings and gifts for them to attain financial breakthrough. This does not work. It is good to give gifts to church and to pay tithes, but these should never be done with the attitude or mentality of getting a payback from God. What if God decides to bless you in other means e.g. good health, obedient children, a happy marriage etc. On the other hand, God will multiply what you have. Remember the teachings in the parable of talents.

f) Look for a trust-worthy person.

To be trusted is a greater compliment than
being loved. (George Mac Donald)

This is difficult nowadays, but it is still possible to find a trustworthy person who can run your business in your absence. If you are employed, for your business to succeed, you must be ready to work more and sleep less. Otherwise, you are likely to lose your investment to unscrupulous employees. One of the best people to run such ventures are spouses. I know of many employed people who have their wives running their side hustles. If both parties are working, be very careful on the choice of business venture, so that you can have a business that you can easily monitor even when the two are working. There so many business opportunities out there, so it is upon you to settle on the one that you can easily manage.

g) Maintain Good Accounting Records.

"It has always been our view that there was poor record-keeping and
someone was stealing wine from Mark." (Douglas Rappaport.)

It is very important that you make it a habit to record all business transactions daily. This will assist in making informed, efficient and precise decisions at any given time. Proper bookkeeping involves maintaining up to date accounting systems, which include recording business transactions as they occur, as well as keeping important receipts or bills for substantiating all expenses incurred on behalf of the business. The records keep the owner informed about their financial position. With the right records, a business owner is able to identify areas for expansion or improvements. These records also comes in handy when the owner wants to secure a loan for business expansion. Additionally, proper analysis of business records can help in making strategic decision of changing business focus. It is crucial to understand that good records shorten the length of time that an audit takes to be completed. They also help the owner to avoid interest and penalties as they make it easier for them to pay the right amount of tax and at the right time.

h) Plan on Expansion.

Vision is the art of seeing the invisible. (Jonathan Swift.)

Learning how to grow your business is not just a worthy goal; growing your business is often a necessity for your business's survival and your economic well-being. There are various methods of growing your business and making your products or services available to a new pool of customers. The most obvious is to open new stores in new locations. New locations can also be virtual, such as a website with an online store. Another good approach is to extend your reach through advertising. Once you have identified a new market, you might find it necessary to advertise in select media that targets that market. If your new market consists of younger demographics, you may want to use social media for advertising. Another important factor that might earn you more customers is a diversification of your products and services. Here you may want to focus on the related needs of your already established market. For instance if you have specialised on making certain beauty products e.g. perfume, you can combine them with lipsticks, roll-ons etc. If you are an artist selling pictures, you might as well sell frames and offer flaming services.

i) Exercise integrity.

Business does not function in a vacuum
of ethics. (Donald Lee Sheppard)

Lack of integrity can pronounce a death sentence to your business. We all have seen it happen countless times, even with organisations considered "too big to fall". A good example in Kenya is the collapse of the Nakumatt Supermarkets, Uchumi Supermarkets among other big ventures. Business leaders who do not conduct themselves with integrity may very well climb to the top of the corporate ladder, but sooner or later, their conduct will make the giants they manage to fall with a thud. Business does not function in a vacuum of ethics. Young people should understand that making huge profits without following due process would eventually lead to destruction.

Donald Lee, the author of "The Dividends of Decency" and CEO of Sheppard Associates, in his article, "Knowing how to Manage Business with Integrity", lists down six benefits of integrity in business as follows:

i. **Better company culture**. If those in leadership positions behave with integrity, and employees do the same, there will be more mutual trust and respect within the organization. This translates to a whole slew of added benefits: flexible work arrangements, improved morale, better communication, and more money left over to celebrate all the hard work employees are doing.

ii. **More satisfied customers.** Operating a business with integrity will make customers feel safe and secure. They will not feel taken advantage of and they will want to keep giving you their business repeatedly. They will recommend you to others and become your greatest advocates.

iii. **Attracting employees with integrity.** In many ways, integrity is a self-fulfilling prophecy. Organizations that value and prioritize integrity will attract employees who do the same. Young people entering the workforce now are especially concerned with working for organizations that behave ethically and are socially aware. Attract top talent by making integrity a key part of your business plan.

iv. **Growth and sustainable profits & improved overall performance.** Prioritizing profits over all else is not a good long-term business strategy (it is not a strategy at all!). Organizations who put profits above integrity risk damaging their relationships and reputation. The dividends of integrity cannot be overstated - it turns out that integrity drives corporate performance.

v. **Avoiding legal trouble.** Repeatedly, we witness companies investing time, effort, and money into reducing fines levied because of them committing infractions instead of behaving in a manner that would have prevented them from incurring the fines in the first place. Sure, you can hire a lawyer, but the best (and cheapest) way to handle legal trouble is to avoid getting into it.

vi. **Positive impact on the community and on society as a whole.** Business in a democracy does not function in a vacuum of ethics. It acts as a vital weave in the fabric of society, shaping the mutual exchange of benefits. Proposing that a business operation is obligated to assume a positive role in the economic and social welfare of the community is not socialist. It is simply good business.

Note.
If you want to go far in business, integrity is key. Business without integrity is hurtful to both the employees who run the venture and the customers who are usually cheated and misused. An entrepreneur's goal should always be, **"to achieve great success in business within the umbrella of integrity."**

Challenge Segment
➢ Some people feel that it is impossible to do business while still in employment. Is this a fact?
➢ If you are lucky to be employed, what are some of the actions that you can take to enhance your savings?
➢ Business without integrity will not take you far. Why?
➢ What are some of the benefits of integrity?
➢ Attitude determines your altitude when it comes to business. How can you adopt positive attitude towards investment?

Great Lessons
❖ If you have to be successful in business, you need to adopt a positive attitude towards investment.
❖ You will not go far, if your business venture is lacking on integrity.
❖ Employed people can use their savings to invest in business.
❖ Procrastination is a dream killer when we come to investment.
❖ To Put God first in all your undertakings is important in business.
❖ Good accounting records is crucial in successful business.
❖ Faith in business without action is dead.
❖ When you start a business, you must be in charge.

Chapter Sixteen

WHAT MAKES
A BUSINESSMAN TICK?

The strength of a man is measured not by where he stands in the times of comfort but where he stands in times of hardship and adversaries. (Martin Luther King)

The never give up mentality.

Most businesspersons will never tell you the failures or struggles they encountered when starting and building their business empires. Most of us are preoccupied by their success stories to the extent that we become blind to the hurdles and challenges that they had to overcome. Jack Ma founder and executive chairperson of Alibaba says, **"Never give up. Today is hard, tomorrow will be worse, but the day after tomorrow will be sunshine"**

Many companies will hardly disclose their failures, unless you ask. This is because "it is not good for business." As we all know, the journey to succesful entrepreneurship is quite tough. There comes a time when the challenges seem overwhelming, a time when some are forced to consider throwing in the towel especially after suffering several setbacks. If this happens, the entrepreneur tends to doubt whether they have what it takes to achieve their dreams and aspirations. Some go to the extent of thinking that their life transforming idea is not viable. Rather than being optimistic, self-doubt and frustrations get into their hearts and despair sets in. If an entrepreneur is not focused, he/she is likely to give up. Nevertheless, for those who push and press on, rewards are just around the corner.

Apparently, the process of moving from the category of underachievers to that of success and prominence is extremely excruciating. The bottom line here is learning from your mistakes, reorganising yourself and forging forward. Jack Ma put it thus, **"The world will not remember what you say, but will certainly not forget what you have done."**

Jack Ma's inspiring story

Ma Yun, a.k.a. Jack Ma is one of those self-made billionaires with **humble beginnings**. He is the founder of the E-commerce giant Alibaba and is a stakeholder at Alipay, its sister company which is an e-payment portal. He is now officially the **richest man in China** with an estimated **net worth of $25 Billion**, on the back of the recent world record $150 Billion IPO filing of his company. Given all of this, Jack Ma only holds a 7.8% stake in Alibaba and a 50% stake in Alipay. Alibaba and Jack Ma, though not household names out of China, **Alibaba is worth more than Facebook, and processes goods more than eBay and Amazon combined!**

This might sound like a story of an arrogant and rich billionaire who has not seen days. However, do not be mistaken by the numbers that you see above, they can fool anyone. As simple as it may sound, Jack Ma has had it hard in his life to get to where he is today. A true rags-to-riches story and definitely one that will inspire you in your darkest days.

Jack Ma was born in Hangzhou, located in the southeastern part of China. He was born and raised along with an elder brother and a younger sister during the rise of communist China and its isolation from the Western regions. His parents were traditional musicians-storytellers who did not make enough to be even considered as middle class during those days.

Former US president Richard Nixon's visit to Hangzhou in 1972 improved the tourism status in his hometown. Jack wanted to make the most of this opportunity. He had always wanted to learn English as a kid. He spent his early mornings riding on his bike to a nearby park, giving English tours to foreigners for free. It was then that he met a girl who nicknamed him 'Jack' because his name was hard to spell for her.

After graduating with a Bachelor's degree in English, he worked as an English teacher at Hangzhou Dianzi University **with a pay of $12 a month!** Now here comes the part where it gets more interesting. Jack Ma is an extremely lucky bloke **who just became a billionaire in a snap**.

However, it is safe to know that rejections are synonymous with Jack Ma. You would not believe the number of times he has been rejected and failed.

During his early childhood, Jack Ma failed in his Primary School examinations, not once, but twice! **He failed thrice during his Middle School exams**. When applying for university after high school, Jack failed the entrance exams thrice, before finally joining Hangzhou Normal University. He even applied and wrote to Harvard University ten times and got rejected each time. This was only during his education!

During and after his Bachelor's degree, Jack tried but failed to get a job anywhere. After three years in the University, **Jack failed to land a job** after applying for 30 times! He recollects in his interview, "When KFC came to China, 24 people went for the interview. Twenty-three people were accepted. I was the only guy who wasn't." He was also among 5 applicants for a job in the Police force, but was turned away with, "No, you're no good." In addition, in his entrepreneurial undertakings, Jack Ma went on to fail on two of his initial ventures. However, that did not stop him in any way of dreaming bigger.

Down, but not out! In one of his interviews, when asked about his rejections, he said, **"Well, I think we have to get used to it. We're not that good."** Overcoming the pain of numerous rejections and treating them as opportunities to learn and grow was what Jack Ma made of it. After finally coming to terms with all of his rejections and failures, Jack Ma visited the US in 1995 for a Government project related to the building of highways. It was then that he was first introduced to the Internet and Computers. Computers were rare in China then, given the high costs associated with them, and Internet or E-mails were non-existent. The first word he searched on the Mosaic browser was 'Beer', and it popped out results from different countries, but no signs of China anywhere. He then searched 'China' and not a single result popped out! He decided it was time for China and its people to get on the Internet.

Finally, **after persuading 17 of his other friends to invest and join him in his new e-commerce startup – Alibaba**, the company began from his apartment. Initially, Alibaba did not have a single penny in investment

103

from outside investors, but they later raised $20 Million from Softbank and another $5 Million from Goldman Sachs in 1999. Building trust among the people of China that an online system of payment and package transfers is safe was the biggest challenge Jack Ma and Alibaba faced, a challenge that Jack will cherish for his lifetime.

Having started **his first successful company at the age of 31** and even after never having written a single line of code or selling something to anyone, Jack Ma runs one of the biggest E-commerce networks in the world. The company went on to grow rapidly, expanding all across the world, quickly growing out of its China shell. Only second to Walmart in terms of sales per year, Alibaba has become the E-commerce giant that Jack Ma has envisioned for it. In an interview, Jack Ma is quoted as saying, "We keep fighting. We keep changing ourselves. We don't complain." Jack Ma said.

Believing in yourself, being persistent in the face of adversities and treating rejections and failures as opportunities to propel yourselves ahead is what Jack Ma's extraordinary life speaks out to the world. Our own Wangari Maathaai put it this way, **"you cannot enslave a mind that knows itself, that values itself, that understands itself."**

Challenge Segment
➤ Entrepreneurship is not a walk in the park. Why?
➤ Jack Ma started his first successful company at the age of 31. What about you?
➤ What can you learn from the numerous failures of Jack Ma in his early years?
➤ Failures and challenges should never enslave your mind from dreaming big. How do you interpret this in a business perspective?
➤ People who embark on business are often criticised and discouraged, even by close relatives. As a graduate, how will you overcome such discouragements?

Big Lessons
❖ Entrepreneurship demands perseverance, handwork and

commitment.

- ❖ It is never too early or too late to start.
- ❖ We should learn to treat our failures as opportunities to propel ourselves ahead.
- ❖ Our past failures will not hinder us from becoming successful in the future.
- ❖ A mind that knows itself, values itself and understands itself cannot be enslaved.
- ❖ Critics and discouraging comments are common for those starting to venture into business but they should never stop you from moving forward.

Chapter Seventeen

BUSINESS NEGOTIATIONS

During a negotiation, it would be wise not to take anything personally. If you leave personalities out of it, you will be able to see opportunities more objectively. (Brian Koslow.)

Negotiation is a process where two or more parties with different needs and goals discuss an issue to find a mutually acceptable solution. Good negotiations contribute significantly to business success as they:

   i. Help your business to build better relationships.

   ii. Help you to deliver lasting and quality solutions to satisfy both parties.

   iii. Help you to avoid future problems and conflicts.

For one to become a good negotiator, he/she ought to be:

   i. Flexible and creative.

   ii. Aware of self and others.

   iii. Professional and good mannered.

   iv. Honest and win-win oriented.

   v. One with good communication skills.

Effective business negotiation is a core leadership and management skill. Its the ability to negotiate effectively in a wide range of business contexts, including deal making, employment discussions, corperate team building, labour/management talks, contracts, handling disputes, employee compensation, business acquisitions, vendor pricing and sales, real estate leases and fulfilment of contract obligations.

The Art of Negotiating.

According to Geoffrey Michael, a freelancewriter specialising in business, finance, Law, negotiating and political analysis, a good business negotiation should consider the following key points.

a) Preparation is Key. Know about the party you are negotiating with so that you can capitalize on your strengths and the party's weaknesses. If the other party is very experienced, that means he also has a history that could contain useful information. If possible, talk to business associates who have dealt with this person before. Many negotiators develop patterns and certain styles that you may be able to use to your advantage. If you are a buyer, make sure you are thoroughly familiar with the product or service that will be the subject of negotiation. If the other party senses you are weak on such details, you may be a prime target for a bluff or another technique designed to create anxiety and uncertainty. Psychology plays a crucial role in your ability to make the most of the other party's lack of preparation and anticipate their next move.

b) Have a price Target/Goal. Most negotiators have a price target or goal in mind before they start. It should be based on realistic expectations considering all the constraints that will undoubtedly surface. These may include budget limits, direction from management, pressure to make sales goals, and a myriad of other external forces. During the course of the negotiation, the goal may change based on changes in scope and other unforeseen actions by either party. While you are ultimate goal should be realistic, this should not constrain your first offer or counteroffer.

c) Understand the Authority of the Negotiator. Before you start the negotiation, ensure that the other party is fully empowered to make binding commitments. You do not want to find yourself in a position where you believe you have struck a deal, only to discover that someone higher in the chain of command must approve your agreement.

d) Always Have a Strategy. There are basic principles that apply to every negotiation. The first offer is usually the most important and the benchmark by which all subsequent offers will be judged and compared. You will never get what you do not ask for, so make your first offer bold and aggressive. The asking price is just that. In addition, the offer price will typically include a pad or margin to give away during negotiations. You want to take all of that and more, so start lower than the seller expects. Do not worry about insulting the other party. As long as your offer is not ridiculous, the other side will continue the negotiations in hopes of settling at a better figure.

e) Never disclose your Budget or other limitations.

As a buyer, do not disclose your budget or other limitations in your negotiating position. A favorite ploy of sales representatives is to reshuffle the product specifications, schedule and other parameters in order to sell you an inferior product to fit your budget. You want the best product you can get for the money you have to spend, so employ an approach that maintains the possibility of spending less than you had originally planned.

f) Give and Take Method.

Always have something to give away without hurting your negotiating position. If you are submitting a price proposal to a buyer, consider inserting decoys and red herrings for the other party to find. For example, if you are bidding a project, consider including some nice-to-have items that are not critical to the success of the project. You could also include spare parts that may or may not be needed in the end. If the buyer takes those items out to reduce the overall cost, you have not lost anything but it may help the buyer reach his price target. Such distractions will help to divert the other party from attacking the meat of your proposal. Employing this strategy must be viewed in the context and in consideration of what other bidders may be doing. If you know that the only way to win the bid is to provide a barebone cost, then this strategy may not be appropriate.

g) Study the non-verbal cues.

Watch for clues such as body movement, speech patterns and reactions to what you say. Be prepared to suspend or cancel negotiations if you feel things are getting nowhere or the other party seems stuck in their position. Indicate your reluctance to continue under those conditions and make the other side wonder if you are ever coming back. If they are on the hook to cut a deal, they will feel the pressure to move. Be patient even if the other party is not. This can be difficult for those with a passion for instant gratification, but the last thing you want is for the other party to think you are under the gun to finish quickly.

h) Have a contractual Standpoint.

From a contractual standpoint, a counteroffer automatically rejects all previous offers. Once an offer is made, you should expect an acceptance or rejection of your offer, or a counteroffer that keeps the negotiation open. If your offer is rejected and you are asked to submit a new and better offer, do not fall into that trap. That would be tantamount to negotiating with yourself, and you should never do this. If the last offer on the table is yours, always insist on a counteroffer to force the other party to move his/her position before you make another offer.

i) Find the Leverage.

In addition to exploiting the other party's weaknesses, concentrate on taking maximum advantage of your strengths. If you are the only source available for a particular product, you have tremendous advantage across the board. If economic conditions have created a market in which the product you are selling is in great demand and low supply, that gives you more bargaining power to name your price. If you are the buyer in a depressed economy, you normally have the advantage of too much supply and lower demand. The current housing situation is a classic example of what happens when supply vastly outweighs the demand and market prices fall dramatically.

Establish a strong foundation early in the process by demonstrating your knowledge and expertise in the subject matter. This may intimidate those on the other side and put them on their heels before they have a chance to establish their own credibility. Playing catch-up in a tough negotiation can be challenging, so it is much better to take the initiative and steer the process in the direction you want.

j) Understand The Offer.   An offer is more than just a dollar amount. It must encompass all of the elements of the bargain and will normally comprise the basis for a contract that formalizes the agreement. If you make an offer without nailing down all of the specifics, you may find out later that there was no meeting of the minds with the other party. The basis of the bargain should include the offer price (in proper denomination), statement of work (scope), identification and quantities of goods or services, delivery schedule, performance incentives (if any), express warranties (if any), terms and conditions and any documents incorporated by reference.

k) Trade one element for another.

Trading one element for another such as a lower price for a more relaxed schedule, is a common tactic. These bargaining chips should be kept in your hip pocket until you need them to close the deal and get the price you want. While your primary focus is normally on price, you should always keep all the other components of the deal in the forefront of your mind. Do not be pressured into accepting boilerplate contracts presented as the "standard of the industry" or something that "we always use." Everything, including the fine print, is open to change. If the other party refuses to alter onerous terms, consider taking your business elsewhere.

l) Be clear in your Negotiation.

To avoid misunderstandings, offers should be presented in writing and include all elements of the bargain. It is a good idea to keep notes containing the rationale for each offer. While these notes will not be disclosed to the other party, they will prove to be invaluable should things go awry and you need to restart negotiations. Part of the process is benefiting from lessons learned and refining your approach and technique. If you work for a company or the government, those notes are usually required to document the negotiated outcome and complete the contract file.

m) Go for a Win-Win Solution. Throughout the negotiation, try to determine what you believe to be an acceptable outcome for the other party. It may be a combination of different things; not necessarily tied solely to price. For example, the delivery date may be the most important thing to the other party, while product quality may be your primary driver.

n) Understand your Negotiator Priorities. Understanding the other side's priorities is just as important as understanding your own, so figure out what you would do if you were in their shoes. When constructing your offers, attempt to satisfy some of their priorities if doing so does not weaken your overall position. Be prepared to give up the little things in exchange for the big things you do not want to concede. Know your limits: how far you are willing to go in all aspects of the deal. While you have the power to influence the negotiation process in your favor, your goal should be to secure a good deal without extracting the last pound of flesh from the other party. This is especially true if you will be negotiating with the same party on a recurring basis. The most effective negotiators are professionals who know their business and do not let personalities and irrational behavior interfere with their mission. They are capable of making the other party believe they got the best deal they could under the circumstances.

o) Goodwill is Crucial. Once the negotiation is completed, you want to be able to work effectively with those in the other party during contract performance. If they are threatened and pounded into submission, they probably will not negotiate with you again, possibly cutting off any future business. While heated confrontation is a common occurrence during negotiations, at some point collaboration and compromise are needed to get a deal.

o) Know how to close the Deal.
Successful negotiation is like horse-trading in that it requires a sense

of timing, creativity, keen awareness and the ability to anticipate the other party's next move. Negotiation is also like chess in that each move should be designed to set up not only your next move, but also several moves down the line. Generally, your moves should get progressively smaller, and you can expect the same from the other party. Always have the end game in mind as you plot your strategy, and be prepared at some point to split the remaining difference. It is almost inevitable when the parties are close but cannot seem to make that last leap to a single number. It is completely arbitrary, but it gets the job done. That is why all the offers leading up to that point are so important: they will set the stage for the final handshake.

Note.
Unless you are negotiating a surgeon fee in a matter of life and death case, nobody is going to die if the deal is closed. So never, be in a hurry to conclude your business deal. On the other hand, avoid making a deal out of desperation. If you are to make it in a successful business venture, you must learn the art of negotiation.

The power in Canada Trade Negotiation
Summary
This case study shows how a weaker negotiating partner can successfully use power negotiation to win a good agreement with a stronger negotiating partner. On October 3, 1987, representatives of Canada and the United States signed The Free Trade Agreement (FTA) after two strenuous years of intense negotiations. Canada could be described as a medium sized economy. Its population is 1/10th the size of the U.S. which is considered an economic superpower in comparison. Canada is economically dependent on the United States. The reason is mainly due to its small domestic market, scattered over a vast geographical locale. More than 75% of its exports go to the U.S. making the U.S. Canada's prime trading partner. By contrast, the U.S. was exporting less than 20% of its products to Canada.

In the 1970's, Canada's economic health rose and fell like the proverbial yo-yo. It was too resource-based and needed to add some revenue to its manufacturing industry to stabilize. A Royal Commission concluded that Canada's only means to achieve this stability was to engage in an open free trade partnership with the United States. The problem was that the United States was not especially interested in such a free trade partnership agreement. The U.S. was in addition also becoming increasingly protectionist during this same period. The result was that Canada was facing a whole host of penalties and countervailing actions against Canadian goods. Canada clearly needed a plan to gain power advantage.

The first step that Canada took was in the form of preparation by developing a succinct plan. The Canadian Prime Minister himself appointed a chief negotiator, Simon Riesman. He established an ad-hoc organization called the trade negotiations office (TNO) which reported directly to the Canadian Government Cabinet and had access to the highest levels of bureaucracy. It established clear negotiation goals and objectives which included a strong dispute resolution mechanism that the Canadians felt were vitally important for their success. In contrast, the United States did not consider the FTA important and let Canada do the entire initial work. The only reason why the U.S. Congress even considered the FTA proposal was that they liked the idea of a bilateral approach to trade and were tired of the previous mechanism that failed to settle a host of trade dispute irritants between the two countries known as the General Agreement on Tariffs and Trade (GATT). It would also allow freer access to other segments of the Canadian economy. President Ronald Reagan decided to fast track the negotiations and appointed Peter Murphy to represent their interests. The U.S. was also concerned about the growing hegemony of the European economy.

Strong differences in interests and approach dogged the negotiations. The Canadians used every advantage available including the use of Summit Negotiation Meetings between the leaders of both countries to emphasize their concerns at every opportunity, yet the political powers in the U.S. dragged their feet to such an extent that the Canadian negotiators walked away from the talks to express their displeasure. This put some heat on the U.S. administrators to the extent that U.S. Treasury Secretary Baker took over the negotiations. Consequently, the talks between the two countries were successfully concluded. Several concessions were made by both countries. The U.S. opened up a larger investment segment in the Canadian economy and removed some of the more time-consuming trade irritants. The Canadians achieved their main goals - freer access to the U.S. economy, while implementing a strong Trade Dispute Resolution Method. The Free Trade Agreement between the two countries created the largest bilateral trade relationship in the world. Canada achieved its objectives because of its detailed planning and the intense focus of its negotiating team despite the asymmetry in power between the two nations.

The Challenge Segment

➤ In a business, more often than not, you have to make a business deal. How would you deal with that?

➤ Even a small business enterprise can win a huge business deal. What lessons do you learn from Canada's success story?

➤ As a business owner, how will you ensure zero exploitation in business deals?

➤ Are negotiation skills or expertise important in business?

The Great Lessons

❖ If you have to win business deals with government and other organisations, you must know how to negotiate.

❖ Avoid getting personal during negotiations: be professional and objective.

❖ With great negotiation, skills and good planning, you can win a big deal despite your size and financial status.

❖ Goodwill is crucial during negotiations: strive to make a long lasting deal.

❖ Always have the best negotiating team engage negotiators.

❖ Research and thorough planning is all it takes to make a good negotiator.

Chapter Eighteen

THE POWER OF
ADVERTISEMENT

*Doing business without advertising is like winking at a
girl in the dark. You know what you are doing, but
nobody else does. (Stewart Henderson Britt.)*

Advertising is the best way to communicate to the customers. Advertising helps inform the customers about brands available in the market and the variety of products useful to them. It can target anybody: kids, young and old.

Why Advertise?

According to business experts, there are four main objectives as to why corporarates conduct advertisement. These include:

- ✓ To conduct a business trial.
- ✓ For business continuity.
- ✓ For brand switching
- ✓ For switching back to business.

a) **Business trial** - This is for those companies that have just started operating. The focus here is to woo customers to like and buy their products and services. The advertiser usually use flashy and attractive ads to make customers look for the products. The ads are also repetitive emphasizing on the quality of the new products in the market.

b) **Business Continuity.** The main objective here is to maintain existing customers. The company focus is to make those customers continue buying or using their services. The advertiser will focus on showing improvement on the products or services in a bid to make them stay.

c) Brand Switching. This usually occurs when two or more companies join in order to address the need in the market or address financial challenges. Because of such factors, brands may sometimes be changed. The advertisers in this case try to convince the customers to switch from the existing brand to the new brand that is better or enhanced.

d) The switch back. - This happens when a company or business enterprise loses customers to competitors. The advert is meant to win them back. This is the hardest advert as winning customers back takes more than a good advert. The company therefore uses price reductions, discounts, repackaging, promotions et al.

The importance of Advertising
Stopping advertising to save money is like
stopping your watch to save time. (Henry Ford)

Advert versus customers. Adverts inform customers of the products available in the market. This helps them to select the one they want based on personal interest, need and affordability.

Advert versus sellers. Adverts help the sellers to increase their sales since their products are able to penetrate more in the market due to awareness created by the ads. It also helps companies to know their competitors and plan accordingly to match their level. It also helps companies to introduce new products in the market.

Advert versus society. Adverts help in educating people or creating awareness on various issues like family planning, child labour, vaccines or vaccination etc. advertisement therefore play a crucial role in the society.

Advertising Tips for Small Scale Businesses
i) Target the right audience. - To master this skill, you need to make a profile of your target customers. You can survey your existing customer base or refer to demographic information.

ii) Target where your customers are. If for example your target audience rages from 20-30 years, a mobile add will do better since most of people in that age bracket are always on their phones. If you are targeting older people from 35 years and above, a radio or television advert will do.

iii) **Track the success of your ads.** You must get results. It is crucial that you evaluate the success of your ads. This will help you to make informed decisions. Digital ads make it easy for you to track the effort. It is possible to know how many people click on your ads and what percentage of those clicks translate to sales.

iv) **Get the timing right.** It is more economical to run your ads campaigns during the most effective time of the year when you are likely to make sales. This it true especially for a small-scale business that lacks the financial muscle of running ads throughout the year. December holidays is one of the best examples since people are willing to spend in buying gifts and other stuffs. If you are selling things like school uniforms or textbooks, you can advertise when the schools are about to open.

v) **Try remarketing.** This involves targeting your ads to your previous customers or people who have visited your website but yet to buy your products. If you add something like a discount, you stand a higher chance of making sales.

Note

The key to effective marketing is consistency in advertisement and constant improvement of products or services through innovation. Once you get your first customers, deliver good quality services. Coming up with innovative methods of improving the quality of your products plays a big role in helping you retain your customer base. Promotions and discounts during the pick season help in establishing goodwill with your customers. It is also important to know that neglected customers are a target of your competitors.

Social Media Advertisement Successful Story
Product: Red Bull (Energy drink.)
Platform Used: Instagram.
About the Company

Consumers have been "given wings" for well over 28 years by Red Bull which ranked #76 on Forbes Most Powerful Brands List in 2015. Their original energy drink can be found in over 170 countries, so it comes as no surprise that the company has sold over 60 billion cans of their famous drink. Since their humble beginnings back in 1987, the brand has since released four new flavors of energy drinks to cater to individual tastes and preferences.

Goal

To drive awareness of the extension of the brand. The goal of their Instagram campaign was based on boosting awareness and sales of their tropical flavored "Summer Edition" energy drink for the Australian market.

Solution

With a firm focus on simplicity and brand building, Red Bull paved the way for their actual campaign with a promotional teaser just before the summer hit. To get audiences focused on the new look of the cans, they incorporated yellow filters across a range of images and videos portraying typical summer days. The brand was twice as likely to be associated with the #this summer hashtag trend as any of its nearest competitors.

Results

- 10-point lift in top-of-mind awareness.
- 9-point lift in favorability.
- 7-point drop in the unconvinced market.
- 1.2 million Consumers reached.

Key Takeaway points.

There is a massive market for campaigns launched on social media sites, and the power Instagram can have in driving engaged users is notable. In order to leverage the full power of a social media campaign on Instagram, you need to understand how consumers use social paths so that you can use them too. Red Bull did this with their #this summer hashtag.

The challenge Segment
➢ What do you think you can achieve through social media adverts?
➢ If you start a business today, when will you start advertising?
➢ Which social media platform do you think is appropriate for your business model?

Big Lessons
❖ There is great gain in advertisement.
❖ When advertising, be specific on the right targetaudience.
❖ Those who think advertisement is a waste of money soon will lose their customer base.
❖ Advertisement benefits are not limited to sellers but extend to the customers and the society in general.

Chapter Nineteen

FACING IT WHEN
YOU HAVE NO AN IDEA
The Kenyans' Hustles

Sometimes you may not have an idea on the kind of business to engage in. That should never worry you because in this chapter I have outlined some various business models that you can start with little money as you figure out your next move.

Movie shop - Ksh 70,000 -100,000. To start a movie shop, you require a stall and equipment. Reliable internet is also key so that you can keep up with emerging videos for clients. Locating your shop close to Universities will obviously place you in a better position as they are willing clients. This business usually targets young people between the ages of 16-35 years. It does well in areas with high population as opposed to low populated areas.

Salon Business - Ksh 50,000-100,000. A salon is defined by its location, services available among other factors. Renting a room and purchasing updated equipment will make your salon stand out. The kind of interior design you choose for your salon will define the class your clients place it. If you offer good services to your customers, they will in turn market your business through the word of mouth.

Car Wash Business ksh 50,000-100,000. Kenyans are buying cars now more than ever. You can easily tap into washing cars for them by starting with at least 15 cars daily. You will require an easy to access yard, reliable source of water, water storage and equipment. The key factor here is the quality of your service plus keeping client's items safe.

Butchery - Ksh 50, 000- 80,000 - Meat is perishable and venturing into it requires ample planning. A good location with potential clients should be your first lookout. Getting a reliable source of meat is also key. Close proximity to a slaughterhouse may do more good.

Money transfer - Ksh 20,000- 50,000. Money transfers hit the country with a bang with almost every Kenyan using MPesa almost on a daily basis. Operating a money transfer business requires a branded shop, an ETR machine, registration and need by clients. Siting a good location for this may not be hard as money transfer is required everywhere every time. To maximize your profit, you can diversify your business by selling mobile phones appliances or any other product that you may find appropriate.

Commercial cleaning - Ksh 80,000 - 100,000. Companies and businesses have long stopped hiring their own cleaners and are now contracting outside companies to get the work done. You will require reliable staff, equipment, and materials to get this done. To get clients, you will need to market your company by letting possible clients know your brand and consider giving you a tender. Use the negotiation skills highlighted earlier in this book to get business.

Boda Boda business - Ksh 50,000- 80,000. Boda Bodas make one of the fastest growing businesses in Kenya with many Kenyans using them for short errands and to reach places they could walk to before. Every town and shopping center has a number of boda-boda operators who ferry people back and forth. To begin this, you need to purchase or rent a motorbike, protective gear, a driving license, and you are ready to go. Treat your customer with dignity. Be clean and polite, and all the customers will be yours.

Online accessories store - Ksh 30,000- 40,000. Technology has enabled so many things to happen with much ease. Operating an online shop only requires you to have a social platform where potential clients can see your brand and make orders. Popular online shops include those selling accessories, clothes, shoes, kitchenware among others. Accompanying your products with pictures is a good marketing strategy in this case.

Children's Daycare - **Ksh 20,000- 30,000**. Kenya has many working people with children who they have to leave during working hours. In the past, these children were left with nannies and house helps but now things are different. Daycares offer parents a chance to leave the children under professional care in their preferred environment. To open a daycare, you have to secure a premise in a children friendly environment, facilities like play things and toys, and to market your brand.

Milk bar - **Ksh 20,000- 30,000**. Milk, being perishable requires careful handling. To venture into this business, you will need a refrigeration system, reliable supply of milk and an identified market gap. With the coming of milk ATMs, you can be able to grow the business to supply milk to a large group of clients.

Green Grocer - **Ksh 2000 - 5000**. This involves selling of vegetables. Kenyans now prefer eating vegetable over meat according to experts. All you need is to identify a perfect site with a good flow of people and identify a good supply of fresh vegetables. To make it more profitable, you can combine your vegetables with fruits.

Online teacher - **Ksh 10000-20000.** If you are good in math, sciences or languages, you can open an online channel in Youtube where you can offer video-recorded lessons and then advertise your channel in social media to get a good audience and following.

Making homemade strawberry Jam and selling. Budget ksh 750/=. You will also need a sufuria (pot), mwiko (wooden stick) and some plastic containers for packaging. With just a little more perfection, you can actually secure a KEBS license and start supplying supermarkets. If you can keep investing more time and creativity into this, there is no reason why you should not grow it into a sustainable business.

Budget Breakdown	Cost
Strawberries	Ksh250 per kilo
Sugar	Ksh100 for 500 grams
Lemons	Ksh100
Packaging pouches	Ksh200
Transport expenses	Ksh100
TOTAL	Ksh750

One kilogram of strawberries will give you approximately 6 cans of jam each weighing 250 grams. You can then sell a 250 gram for Ksh200 making at least Ksh1, 200. Note that you can always expand your profit margins by planting the strawberries yourself.

Selling wall papers (Budget: Ksh1, 800). If making strawberry jam sounds inapplicable, you might want to put your in-born interior design knowledge to good use. Most people live in houses with a dull paint done by their property owners. A number of them would like to have the exterior looking better – but without necessarily repainting it. This is where wallpapers come in handy. You simply get ready-made wallpapers either from local wholesalers or by importing from countries such as china.

Budget Breakdown	Cost
Wall Paper Roll	Ksh1,600 per 10 meters
Other expenses	Ksh200
TOTAL	Ksh1,800

You can sell each roll for Ksh3, 500 and include a Ksh1, 000 as installation charges. That translates to more than double the profit. The more aggressive you are, the more sales you can make and the more revenue you can generate from this.

Selling black coffee (Ksh 6,600). If you live in towns like Nairobi, I am sure you have come across people who sell black coffee in matatu termini. Have you ever stopped to inquire how much they make per day?

Well, at it turns out, this venture is one of those "opportunities dressed in rags" kind of things. For starters, you will require a 10-litre tea urn, some disposable plastic cups and well … a bit of hard work.

Budget Breakdown	Cost
Thermos Flask	Ksh5,000 for a 10 litre tea urn
Disposable plastic cups	Ksh1,000
Sugar	Ksh400 per Kilo
Coffee	Ksh200
TOTAL	Ksh6,600

As long as you are willing to give it your best, there is no reason why you should walk away with less than Ksh1, 000 per day in profits. How? You might want to ask. Well, a 10 litre coffee urn contains 65 x 150ml cups of coffee. Sell each cup at Ksh10 and you will make Ksh. 650 per flask.
If you can make three trips per day – once in the morning and twice in the evening, we can talk about Ksh. 650 x 3 = Ksh1, 950. Subtract the cost of water, sugar and coffee and you realize you can make a cool Ksh1, 500 per day.

Making jewellery from bones (ksh1, 010). Carving jewelry out of beef and camel boiled bones. You collect waste bones from restaurants and slaughterhouses. Sounds like a "chokora's" street urchins job…right. Not until you realize how much potential, it has. Here is the drill. You sharpen them with a circular blade, smooth them with a sand paper, boil them using hydrogen peroxide to remove oil, apply candle wax on them (in pattern) and then dye the bones for one hour. Finally, you design them into either a necklace, beads, bracelets, rings or even earrings.

Budget Breakdown	Cost
Bones	Free or purchase at a small price
Hydrogen Peroxide	Ksh500
Blades and sandpaper	Ksh500
Candles	Ksh10
TOTAL	Ksh1,010

As with any other design business out there, this business rewards the creative mind. So if you are not ready to sit down for hours coming up with some nice concepts; do not risk it. If done right, this has the potential to make you a force to reckon with in the multi-billion jewelry industry.

Chia seeds farming (ksh10, 000). You will be surprised to hear how this little, wonder seed is causing ripples across the world. In fact, just recently, chia wholesalers in Europe were sold out. Why? Because the seed has many health benefits ranging from omega oil to protein supply. With a fast growing market, you can start a small farm to take advantage of this opportunity. It grows in moderately warm areas with well-drained soil e.g. places like Nakuru, Uasin Gishu and Western Kenya. Best of all, the crop thrives organically and you need no fertilizer or pesticide to sustain it.

Budget Breakdown	Cost
Chia seeds	Ksh4,000 for two kilos
Farming cost	Ksh6,000
TOTAL	Ksh10,000

You only need 2 kilograms of it to establish a quarter acre. That will in turn give you a harvest of 75 kilograms after just 3 months. With each Kilogram fetching Ksh. 2, 000 in the market, it means you can comfortably raise Ksh150, 000.

Car Boot Sales (Ksh12, 000). You have been fired, but still have a personal car loan to finance. Do not panic. You can convert that car into a business by making car boot sales. It is very simple; you identify a few fast moving goods, transport them with your car to crowded places or busy streets and sell from the boot. Some fast moving goods include chicken eggs, used toys, traditional vegetables and exotic fruits. The advantage of car boot sales over a permanent shop is that it allows you to move from one place to another. You can also avoid a bulk of county council costs when operating this way.

Budget Breakdown	Cost
Products to sell	As little as Ksh10,000
Fuel and car expenses	Ksh1,000
Any other	Ksh 1,000
TOTAL	Ksh12,000

Making beaded sandals and handbags (ksh3, 870. You need beads. A kilogram of beads goes for Ksh370/= at Kariakor Market in Nairobi and is enough for an entire handbag and a small pouch that you can sell for as much as Ksh3, 000. This represents a profit of Ksh 2,230. You will also need to take a few days to learn the art of beading (around 4 days). Luckily, for you, our very own success story, Ms. Cleopatra Wanjiku, is always on hand to offer training on this. You can find her on her face book page and plan for a session or two.

Budget Breakdown	Cost
Beads	Ksh370 per kilo
Training	Ksh3,000 (may vary)
Needles & strings	Ksh500
TOTAL	Ksh3,870

As a creative art, beadwork gives you the freedom to set the price. You can therefore rake in anything from as little as Ksh. 1, 000 per day to as much as you want depending on your entrepreneurial prowess.

Making Beads From Scratch You do not just need to settle at the idea of making beaded sandals and handbags. You can actually make the beads yourself and supply them to other fashion designers. All you need is to acquire some polymer clay (the one used by urban kids to make mound) which you can use to mound different bead designs. Luckily, for you, there are not many Kenyans doing this and you can therefore take full advantage of the market dynamics. Where do you get polymer clay in Kenya? Well, it is readily available in supermarkets and bookshops. Alternatively, you can import it in bulk.

Budget Breakdown	Cost
Oven-bake clay	Ksh100 per bar of clay
Clay sculpting tools	Ksh1,500
Needles & strings	Ksh500
Polymer clay oven	Ksh10,000
Labour	Ksh200 per labourer per day
TOTAL	Ksh11,800

The venture that depends on one's creativity. Returns may vary from as little as Ksh1, 000 per day to much more depending on economies of scale.

Processing and selling natural oils. You do not need a whole factory along Mombasa road to start producing oils. You simply need to invest in an oil press machine and a few raw materials like avocado, macadamia, sunflowers and chia seeds. Things like avocadoes are readily available in most parts of the country and you can obtain them at throwaway prices. You dry them up and then squeeze them using the machine to produce pure, organic oil. Once you get the oil, you can package it in bottles and supply to your clients. With the need for quality skin care and demand for 100% natural oil emerging, you can rival for a sizeable pie of this lucrative industry right from your living room.

Budget Breakdown	Cost
Automatic cold press machine	Ksh50,000
Raw materials	Ksh1,000
Packaging	Ksh5,000
TOTAL	Ksh56,000

Four avocadoes can produce 50ml of pure oil. You can sell this oil for as much as Ksh100. Yet each avocado would cost you about five bob, which amounts to Ksh. 20 in total. A small set-up can produce and sell 1 litre of avocado oil per day. This loosely translates to Ksh2, 000 in sales. The sales can increase further if you approach supermarkets and cosmetic shops in your area.

Other jobs out there include:

i. Dance instructor.
ii. Script writing.
iii. Motivational speaker.
iv. T-shirt Designer.
v. Photographer.
vi. Freelance writing
vii. Web designing
viii. Booksellers
ix. Berber shop.
x. Sales and marketing of products.
xi. Clothes making or designer.

Note.

As you can see, there is no limit as to what business you can engage in. With money as little as your relatives give you for pocket money, you can always start a business. So do not sit there and complain. Get up and do something.

Making it From the Scratch
How Jimmy Tune Fondo Started a Courier
Company From Nothing

It all started while Fondo was on internship in Mombasa. He organized an event that flopped, and that is what opened his eyes to an opportunity to make money and create employment for himself and others. He started Crosstown Courier Ltd, a mail delivery company based in Mombasa County. This young Kenyan started with zero money and now he is a successful entrepreneur behind the birth of Crosstown Courier Ltd.

"I once volunteered at the Ministry of Education, Mombasa County during my third year in university. I was part of the organizing team that put together the Mombasa County education stakeholder's forum. We printed thousands of invitation letters that were meant to go to all education stakeholders in the county. Two weeks to the event, we had only received a handful responses. We went into a panic. Upon investigation, we discovered that the messengers we had tasked to make the deliveries had outsourced the job to third parties. They could not account if all the letters had been delivered. The long and short of the story is that the event was poorly attended and we lost a lot of money. The event was a flop. I was very disappointed. After the traumatic experience, I thought… what if I had a bicycle and delivered the letters myself? Perhaps the event would not have been a flop!" That is how Crosstown Courier Ltd was born.

"I picked a company name that I feel communicates. You do not need to think too hard. When you read or hear 'Crosstown Courier', it gives you a hint of what we do. We officially launched the business on 1st November 2014 after sweat, blood and tears and the challenges I faced. A good business idea is one thing. Executing the idea is a different thing.

Challenges.

"I faced many challenges when I started. I will highlight the two major ones and explain how I dealt with them. The first challenge I faced was capital. I started the business as a third year campus student surviving on the little pocket money my parents gave me. I really needed a bicycle to run errands but I did not have any money even to buy a cheap one. However, I was very determined to get my business going. Therefore, I convinced a friend who was a night guard to lend me his bicycle. I was born and brought up in Watamu village, Kilifi County, in a place called Timboni. Some think that people from the Coast are lazy. I am not."

"The second headache was gaining trust from clients. You can imagine a third year student convincing clients that he will actually deliver their parcels. Many clients were hesitant that their packages would reach their destination on time and secure. It was like pulling teeth! To overcome this challenge, I started asking clients who had given me business to give me a service satisfactory recommendation letter. This is what I used while approaching new clients. The tactic worked like magic. Since I started the business in 2014, we have invested KSh 370,000. This was money from Swiss Re Foundation through Aiducation International, an organisation that offers merit based high school scholarships and support start-ups. "

Business Objective

" For me, the objective of starting Crosstown Courier Ltd was to replace the old inefficient messenger service and offer a reliable delivery service in Mombasa. We are creating an affordable and reliable delivery system."

Best Seasons

"The busiest season for us is during celebrations. We receive many orders for shopping and food deliveries. We balance by signing long-term contracts with companies to cover us during the dry seasons. I am proud that in the last two years, the business has really grown."

Number of Employees

"Currently, we have six full time employees plus three who work on a part time basis. I hire people who can share our vision and enjoy working in the courier business. All our staff are vibrant youths. I laugh every time I think that I started with a borrowed bicycle. The bicycles have distinguished us from the rest. Our staff use bicycles to get their way around Mombasa City. We save on time compared to our competitors who have invested in vehicles and waste a lot of time in traffic. In addition, maintaining a bicycle is very cheap."

What about Innovation?

"We use electric bicycles. We have also made the lives of our clients very easy through our app. They can book deliveries online. It will be even easier as they can use a delivery app that we will be launching in a few weeks. The App is a game changer, a very big deal for us."

What about Expansion?

"We are collaborating with restaurants in Mombasa to add their food menus in the App. Other business partners who will be on our App include gas suppliers and online shops. This strategy will increase our sales by 50%. I see a very bright future for the business. That is what gives me sleepless nights. We are currently in the process of buying our first three electric bikes. They will be delivered by the end of October 2016. With the bikes, we will improve our delivery time and it will be easy for the delivery staff to move from one zone to another. Buying electric bikes is part of our green entrepreneurship concept."

Advice to upcoming entrepreneurs

Four pieces of advice to aspiring entrepreneurs from Jimmy Tune:

i.   If you have a passion for something or an idea, do not wait. Go ahead. Start with what you have. Most people procrastinate because they want to have everything before starting. There is no perfect time to start. Start with what you have. Other things will find you along the way.

ii. Believe in the idea yourself first. Be passionate about it. Nobody will buy an idea from you if you do not even believe in it.

iii. You will fail. Be ready to fail. Not once, not twice. Many times. The most important thing is how soon you get up, dust yourself and stand. Keep trying. Failing is good because it makes you gain an experience of a lifetime.

iv. There are many people/organisations willing to support young entrepreneurs not only in Kenya but also all over the world. Rise up and be counted.

The challenge segment

➢ Which business model from the list given suits your passion?
➢ Do you trust your business ideas? Why or why not?
➢ Do you think there is a perfect time to start a business?

Big Lessons

❖ Start with what you have: do not wait for big money.
❖ Believe in yourself and your ideas and get started.
❖ Do not get discouraged by mistakes but learn from them and move on.

Conclusion.
"Blaming others for your situation takes time and energy from improving yourself."

Dealing with a negative person is very difficult. Blamers are a type of people who have an inflated sense of self. They never take responsibility for anything or admit their mistakes. They immediately blame everything wrong that happens around them or to them, whether it's their own fault or not, on other people in their life. For example, if they get involved in a car accident, the other driver is to blame for distracting them. If they cannot get a job, it is always because the government or another tribe or the panel in the interview did not know their jobs. If they cannot make it in a relationship, it is always the other partner.

Now after reading this book, I expect you to start taking responsibility. Stop blaming others for your failures and giving excuses as to why you cannot make it in life. You have a DNA of success implanted into you by God. Avoid this song of 'I was not well educated, I am from a single family, I come from an abusive home, my father is a drunkard, I am an orphan', et al. Spare yourself some energy, and instead of complaining, start focusing on what you can do to change your lemon to lemonade.

The same applies to those who are afraid of taking risks in engaging in business or those who have given up in life because they cannot secure white-collar jobs. God has given us energy, brain and talents to pursue our dreams, and he expects us to work towards that. God's great promise to us is, "I will bless the work of your hands." Therefore, whatever you decide to do, just remember this promise.

Finally, I am sincerely thankful for your time and I hope that by the time I release my next book on business matters, you will have started something. Good things are yet to come in your life and I believe you have the right DNA to lead a successful and fulfilling life.

You can also check my other books to get more inspiration about life,: "The Great Truth About God" and "Dating Mathematics" for those who are dating or have children of a dating age. God bless you.

The End.

BIBLIOGRAPHY

1.   A practical guide to getting what you want, when you want it, at the price you want.https://www.entreprenuer.com.cdn.amproject.org

2.   The power in a Canadian Trade.Negotiations.com/case/power-negotiation

3.   Ten simple ideas you can start with as little as ksh 1000 capital. Kuzabiashara.co.ke/blog/simple start

How young Kenyan started a successful business.https://www. tuko.co.ke/219567-this-young-kenyan-started-money-a-successful-entreprenuer.html.

Managing business with integrity https://www.businessknowhow.com/ manage/business-integrity.htm

Kenya Unemployment Statistics.Kenya-unemployment https://www. statista.com

4.   Tear Jerking Story of Kelvin Ochieng.Tear-jerking story of kelvin Ochieng standardmedia.co.ke

5.   Importance of Innovation in Business. https://www.viima.com. cdn.amproject.org

Chamas with wealth and Influence.https://mobile.nation.co.ke/lifestyle/ chamas

Importance of Business Monitoring.https://www.whistl.co.uk/news/ theimportance-of-business-monitoring-and-rep

Innovative Man invent Candle.Kenya.co.ke/news/41712-innovative-man-invent-candle-curbs-malaria.

Profitable Farming Ventures on just a ¼ acre of land in Kenya.https:// blog.kuza.io/8-profitable-farming-ventures-on-just-1/4- acre-of- land-in-Kenya.

13   How I made my first Million in Farming. Standardmedia.co.ke/ article/2001229062/

14   Women supporting women. https://medium.com/verve-up/ womansuportingwomen-kenyan-women